09 1,1

Praise for

G000075082

"This is a fascinating and thought-p
nurture our children's learning. Full (
learn and useful strategies to teach children, it is an invaluable resource for
parents and educators alike."
David Malam, Head Teacher

"This book is compelling, enlightened and insightful. Emma Sargent's mix of
easy-to-understand theory, practical tips and stories all help to make this an
excellent guide book for anyone who is interested in communicating with
and helping children (and adults actually). I read it in one sitting! Forget all the
other parenting books. If you follow Emma's advice, you won't need them."
Sally Bibb, author

"Having worked with Emma over the past eight years, I can happily testify
that she makes this book as accessible, practical and powerful as the work
she has done for me in business. Parents out there – buy it!"
**Simon Kimble, Managing Director and organiser of the
Parenting Show and father of four**

"So often, I look at my children and wonder what on earth is going on in
their heads. I know that they are struggling with something but they find it
difficult to find the words. *Flying Start* showed me how to find out, so that I can
help them effectively. More importantly, unlike other parenting books, I can
help them learn how to help themselves. This is a uniquely practical book."
Louise Austin, mother of two

"Emma's work with my daughter made a difference to how she learns her
spellings and how confident she feels about tackling them. The speed and
degree of change I saw in an hour's session made me want to learn more and
try out more of these techniques myself – it has been fantastic. They are easy
to learn and use and can make a really big difference to everyday family life."
Kate Atkinson, mother of two

Flying Start

Coaching your children for life

Emma Sargent

CYAN

 Marshall Cavendish
Editions

Copyright © 2006 Emma Sargent

First published in 2006 by:

Marshall Cavendish Editions
An imprint of Marshall Cavendish International (Asia) Private Limited
A member of Times Publishing Limited
Times Centre, 1 New Industrial Road
Singapore 536196
T: +65 6213 9300
F: +65 6285 4871
E: te@sg.marshallcavendish.com
Online bookstore: www.marshallcavendish.com/genref

and

Cyan Communications Limited
119 Wardour Street
London W1F 0UW
United Kingdom
T: +44 (0)20 7565 6120
E: sales@cyanbooks.com
www.cyanbooks.com

The right of Emma Sargent to be identified as the author of this work has been
asserted by her in accordance with the Copyright, Designs and Patents Act 1988.

All rights reserved

No part of this publication may be reproduced, stored in a retrieval system or
transmitted in any form or by any means including photocopying, electronic,
mechanical, recording or otherwise, without the prior written permission of the
rights holders, application for which must be made to the publisher.

A CIP record for this book is available from the British Library

ISBN-13 978 981 261 828 3 (Asia & ANZ)
ISBN-10 981 261 828 7 (Asia & ANZ)
ISBN-13 978-1-904879-67-1 (Rest of world)
ISBN-10 1-904879-67-5 (Rest of world)

Printed and bound in Great Britain

To Thomas and Hannah
with all my love

Contents

Acknowledgements

My biggest thank you goes to Tim, my wonderful husband, who has been so encouraging, helpful and inspiring.

Big thank-yous go to everyone who has helped me and especially to:

John Overdurf and Julie Silverthorn, who were there at the moment I realised I should write this book and who have been mentors to me. I could not have written this without the time I have spent studying with them. Much of the content is based on things I learned with them and adapted from their work.

Sid Jacobson, whose workshops fired up a passion in me and who has been incredibly generous.

Robert Dilts who kindly gave me permission to use his Spelling and Maths strategies.

Michael Carroll, who has given me kind and valuable feedback.

All the other people who work in this field with integrity and passion.

Our marvellous friends Claire and Sean who sat up late into the night reading draft copies. Their comments have been invaluable and the process provided us all with yet more things to laugh about together!

Susie Ducker, one of the wisest people I know, who gave Thomas and Hannah the most incredible start to education at her Montessori nursery.

My parents who have provided much appreciated practical grandparent support that made it possible for me to find time to write.

Everyone who contributed with their stories. My apologies to those who provided me with stories that I wasn't able to fit in. Names have been changed.

Everyone who has made encouraging comments and been enthusiastic about this project. Every single comment has contributed to my motivation.

All at Cyan Communications for making this happen.

And most of all to Thomas and Hannah, to whom this book is dedicated.

Introduction
Once upon a time...

I do my best as a mother. Sometimes that's great and sometimes it's not very good at all. I have two children: Thomas, eight, and Hannah, six-and-a-half. I am also a coach and trainer in the field of communication and personal development. As the children have grown older, I have realised that almost everything I do in my work life is applicable to my home life. This book is the bringing together of the two main parts of my life, the one informing the other.

For me, being a parent is the most challenging job I've ever had. It's like being on a rollercoaster; at times wonderful, fun, joyous, and at other times frustrating, monotonous and worrying. It's also something for which I am extremely grateful. I have learned a great deal from my children in their young lives, including a lot about myself, some of which I would have preferred not to have learned! I am continually learning as we grow together, and the path is not always smooth.

When I became a part-time working mother, I struggled with a range of emotions common to many working mothers. I felt guilty about leaving the children with a nanny, even though we could not have wished for a more wonderful nanny. I felt selfish for not wanting to give up doing the work that I love. I wanted to be with the children and resented parting from them (it was often me crying at the front door, not them!). I felt tired a lot of the time, trying to juggle all the areas of my life and, as far as I was concerned, not really managing to do it very well. So, it was an epiphany when I realised that the very nature of the work that I do is making me a better mother than I might otherwise have been. Let me explain.

I have spent over fifteen years working in the fields of learning, coaching, communication and other personal development. In my work, I help people to become self-aware, develop strategies to solve their own problems, and get what they want from their life. Over the years my clients have given me lots of examples of how the work I am doing with them has impacted on their family life; how they have used some of the techniques with their children with extremely positive results.

As my first child, Thomas, got to about three years old I realised that the skills I was teaching adults were applicable, even at that tender age. I couldn't believe some of the things I was able to do with him and what a difference it made to him. I have been amazed at being able to apply coaching skills to children as young as that to help them with nightmares, worries, learning new things, overcoming fears, dealing with arguments, encouraging good behaviour and most excitingly, watching them as they become aware of their internal world and the choices that that awareness gives them. There is no age limit to the usefulness of these skills.

Here's an example of the empowering nature of self-awareness even when you are seven. Thomas gets frustrated very easily if he doesn't understand something straight away. He also gets frustrated pretty much every time he sits down in front of certain types of homework. On this particular day, he was having a go at a fairly simple logic problem when he got stuck. It was one of those "have a go at this everyone" problems you glibly chuck at the family that you think is going to be engaging and fun, and then you wish you hadn't! As soon as he got stuck, I saw his frustration appear, which meant that it was game over as far as his ability to think clearly and creatively was concerned. The rest of the family tried to explain it to him, but of course he wasn't in the humour to hear or understand anything. I said to him gently, "When I get frustrated, it's like a dark grey fog comes down in front of my eyes, and I know that it is hard for me to carry on thinking. What happens to you?"

Thomas: My fog's not grey, it's red.

Me: So it's red.

I used a very interested tone, partly because I was genuinely interested and partly because I really wanted to encourage him to tell me more. Repeating his words also helped because he felt heard.

Thomas: Yes. And it's like a curtain that closes.

Me: Wow. So, when *I* understand and can think clearly, it's bright in my head, sort of white. What's yours?

Thomas: It's bright green. And actually there are lights too. When I start to understand, I can see a green light through the red curtain.

Bear with me reader! I know this sounds completely bizarre.

Me: So what can we do to make sure that you "stay green" when you are doing your homework and trying to understand things?

Thomas: Well, maybe I could look at something green like grass.

We then thought of all sorts of ways that he could "stay green" which will help him when he does his homework.

I must confess that when he answered my question, I was as amazed as you might be right now. I just made sure that I stayed interested and kept asking him about his internal experience. Now, he spends a few moments thinking about the colour green before approaching any task that used to frustrate him. How empowering for him to know that he can manage his moods with a simple technique that is unique to him.

Increasingly, we seem to be living in a world where it is fine to blame everyone else for our problems: our parents, the government, our teachers, even our genes. I would like to live in a world where people take responsibility for themselves and their behaviour and believe that life is about always learning.

I have learned over the years that there are some very simple things that we, as parents, can do to help our children. So often simple techniques, which should be known by and available to us all, are shrouded in the mysterious world of jargon, making them beyond our reach. When I have told friends about these approaches, they have encouraged me to write about them so that they are accessible to everyone. That is my aim.

I met a woman called Lindsay recently. She has a seventeen-year-old daughter, Corinne. When she was about thirteen she started retching and sometimes being physically sick before school. It happened, on average, three out of the five school days per week. This went on for FOUR years, during which time she stopped eating breakfast altogether in attempt to stop the sickness. Imagine what that must have done for her concentration at that important time for growth in a young person's life.

Lindsay was driving her to college just a couple of months ago when Corinne asked her to stop the car so that she could be sick. When she got back into the car, Lindsay said, "Corinne, this has got to stop." "Mum, I know," she replied. "There's a counsellor at college and I'm going to go and see her." It only took a couple of sessions for the counsellor to find out that Corinne was making herself sick with anxiety about having the *right books for the day's lessons*. How did it start? It all started when her teacher bellowed at her in front of the class just once too often for not having the right books for the day.

When I remarked that it was amazing that she had kept it up for four whole years through changes of teachers and even changing schools, Lindsay agreed. She said that she was a bit hurt that she hadn't been able to help her daughter. She said to me, "Nothing I said to her made any difference." I pointed out to her that usually it's not what we SAY that makes a difference, it's what we ASK. Lindsay looked at me as if I had hit her over the head with a spade: "Oh my God, you're right. I didn't know how to find out."

This book is dedicated to transferring the skills of coaching to help develop your children; help them understand how they do things, overcome their problems, learn well and communicate effectively. How are they organising their thoughts so that they feel and behave in a certain way? What are they thinking about that enables them to be so good at mental arithmetic? What are they thinking about that means that they can't bring themselves to jump off the side of a swimming pool? This is exciting stuff.

I will share simple strategies and show you a way of teaching your children to think which will help them to overcome every day obstacles such as not wanting to do homework, arguing with parents or friends, or worrying about something. It will also help them to know and get more of what they want out of life. I started my own personal development when I was nearly thirty – it was only then that I became really aware of what's important to me, what motivates me and how I create my own reality and how I limit myself. I am happy to say that it is very different for my children.

The aim is to nurture independence in our children, so that they can truly think for themselves now, and in the future. Helping our children develop self-awareness and personal responsibility is a precious gift for the next generation.

However, my experience, and also that of my friends, is that our children seem to be put on this earth specifically to test us in every way possible, press every button and provide us with an emotional rollercoaster to ride on a daily basis! This can leave us feeling frustrated, tired, and as if parenthood is a thankless task. When we feel like this, we can find ourselves behaving in a way that is unhelpful to both ourselves and our children.

On the other hand, we also have times when everything is going well, when we feel great, and our children are really engaged with us and whatever we are doing at the time. We all have examples of using a particular approach to deal with certain behaviour, and being delighted with our success. The question is: how can we get more of the success?

The fact is we need to learn how to be our own coach first, becoming aware of both our successes and shortcomings so that we can truly give the best of ourselves to the precious years that we are privileged to spend with our children, helping to shape their future.

So, although this book is primarily for your children, it is also for you.

1

What's it all about?

Becoming a great coach

Think back to when you were a child for a moment. What was it like for you the night before your birthday? There were presents for you. You knew there were because you had seen shopping bags and there had been secret conversations between your family members. You wake up early with excitement on the morning of your birthday. The rest of your family wish you happy birthday and give you your presents. You have no idea what could be in the parcels. You choose one that is a funny shape. "I wonder what's in there . . . ." You feel the parcel all over, prodding and poking it. Finally you begin to unwrap it . . .

Curious? That's what you need to be as a coach – **curious**. The more curious you can be, the more successful you will be in understanding others.

The more you watch and listen to people, the more you are able to understand them and the less judgemental you become. The more you notice, the more fascinating your interactions become and the more you discover.

What does a coach do?

A coach is someone who helps others reach their potential by helping them to become self-aware, develop a sense of responsibility for their actions, build a positive self-image, change behaviours that are not useful to them, overcome problems that hold them back, work out what they want and then help them get there.

Through adding the role of coach to our children as part of parenting, we teach them a way of being from an early age that will stay with them for the rest of their lives, and a set of valuable skills. Some of these are:

- Developing self-esteem and a positive self-image.
- Knowing how to learn effectively.

- Being able to work out what they want and achieve it.
- Solving their own problems.
- Taking responsibility for what happens to them in their life.
- Being able to form successful relationships.
- Dealing with conflict in a positive way.
- Being able to understand the effect they have on others.
- Being able to think for themselves.

What skills do you need to be a coach?

A good coach has many skills, but the three key skills are: the ability to notice behaviour, give feedback and ask questions. An excellent coach also has an overriding attitude of curiosity.

Noticing behaviour

Often, if we ask someone how they do something that they are very good at, they can't tell us. That is because they are naturally good, and have never had to consciously think it through. For example, Tony is good at remembering names at a party. If you were to ask him how he does it, the most likely answer would be: "I don't know. I just can."

In order to make someone aware of what they are doing, you need to be able to notice it first. Coaches need to be good at watching out for how someone is doing something and small signs that tell them how they are thinking. Somebody's eye movements are a good indicator of **how** they are thinking; valuable information to feed back to them to help them become aware of their thinking processes. A good coach would be able to notice how Tony is organising his thinking in order to remember names and with some well-directed questions, help him to discover how he does it.

Coaches need to be able to really listen, not only to what someone is saying, but **how** they are saying it. Noticing when they use language that limits them is important. It helps them to become aware of their internal thinking processes that may be preventing them from getting what they want. If a coach is good at listening in this way, they can then ask insightful questions that help the individual reach their own solutions.

Giving feedback

Becoming aware of what we do is the first step in being able to change or improve. All high-performing sports men and women have coaches who make them aware of what they are doing. Sometimes, it is the smallest thing that makes the difference between winning and losing. For example, a coach might notice that a specific shoulder muscle is being used in a swimming turn in a certain way, which, when changed, takes a few tenths of a second off his performance. The swimmer could not possibly have discovered this by himself.

It is the same with everything that we do. If we are given feedback on our behaviour, it makes us aware; and awareness gives us choices. We do not have a choice of changing if our behaviour is out of our conscious awareness.

This awareness restores choice and is the first step towards changing our behaviour, if we want to. Just as it is useful to understand what we want to change, it is equally useful to understand how we do things that we are good at so we can do more of them and improve them still further.

Asking questions

The ability to ask good questions is an incredibly powerful skill. I wish that I had been taught how to ask questions at school, rather than leave it to luck. Sometimes, just one question, carefully chosen in a coaching situation, can make someone's problem disappear.

Questions can be the key to helping someone to think through a problem, think through what they want and help them achieve it.

Using these skills with your children will encourage them to understand themselves and fulfil their potential.

In order to use the skills effectively, coaches also need:

1 A framework.
2 An understanding of how people process information, communicate, and organise their thoughts to create their unique view of the world. Chapter 3 is devoted to exploring this process.

A framework for coaching

Why use a framework? Life does not fit into a framework. Real problems don't neatly fit into a framework. Real children do not fit neatly into a framework. Every day life can be a bit of a messy business. So why use one?

The purpose of having a framework is to make sense of the messiness of life more easily. Ironically, a framework allows you space to be creative and flexible in your approach. I learned this when I went on a course a few years ago to become qualified as a facilitator of a creative problem-solving process. The first part of the course was taken up with us being on the receiving end of the process. We spent hours being really creative as a group, making random and at times wild free-word and idea associations that I found rather liberating! What I was surprised to discover later was that it was the strict framework that the course leader was applying, that enabled us to be creative. And so it is with coaching.

I use a very simple framework in my thinking, wherever I am. It has become second nature now. It can be applied to almost anything from helping a small child understand consequences, to coaching a chief executive; from helping a child to do something they don't want to do, to using it as a sales process in a commercial environment.

The Framework

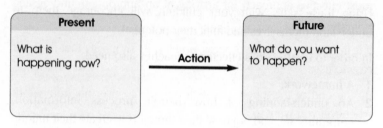

Present		Future
What is happening now?	**Action** →	What do you want to happen?

1   The **Present** refers to the situation as it is now, which could be:

- A problem or issue confronting the parent or child.

- An awareness of your or your child's knowledge and skills as they stand, accompanied by a desire to develop or change in some way.

2   The **Future** refers to what you or your child wants: your outcome.

3   **Action** refers to the steps you need to make to achieve your outcome.

The sequence of **Present–Future–Action** may seem obvious. I want to stress that it is essential to know what someone wants *before* making suggestions or offering solutions.

Have you ever had a problem and discussed it with a friend? You tell them a bit about your problem and they start to offer you solutions because they care about you and don't want you to have the problem anymore. You think about the solutions as they suggest them, but none of them seems to quite fit. This is because you may not be sure about what you want. When we have a problem we find it difficult to focus on what we want instead of the problem.

The most useful help that your friend could give you is to help you to work out what you really want. Once you know that, it is likely that you will know what action to take yourself.

WHAT'S IT ALL ABOUT?

Since coaching is a future-orientated approach to change, we need to always focus on what either we or our child wants as this is the most effective approach for arriving at an appropriate and agreed solution.

It is in essence a simple process, and it is its simplicity that makes it easy to use.

By the end of this book, you will be able to use this framework whenever you want to.

2

Starting with you

Being the parent you want to be

If you want to coach others, you first need to be aware of your own strengths and weaknesses. It is an important step in understanding the impact you may have on others.

You are your child's most powerful role model from the moment they are born. Children are such incredible sponges when it comes to learning.

How often has one of your children said something that may have surprised you, only for you to realise it was a direct quote from you? I heard a great story recently of a little boy (now a grown man of fifty!) who, aged five, had to go into hospital to have his tonsils out. He was in a hospital run by nuns who were extremely caring and gentle. Imagine their surprise when his answer to, "What would you like to drink?" was, "I think I'll have a small sherry." Straight from the mouth of his mother!

We wonder sometimes where on earth our children's character traits come from, only to be met with raised eyebrows and amused grins from our partners and friends.

There is enough evidence around to indicate that what happens at home has an enormous impact on a child's development. Our children are not just learning how to do things at home, they are learning ways of being in the world. They are forming their opinions, working out what's important to us and them, how to fit into society, how to interact with friends, what being part of a family means and so on. We must be aware of the messages they are getting from us, both spoken and unspoken, and the beliefs about themselves and the world around them that they are forming as a result.

Take as an example, parents who talk about their children negatively within their earshot as if the child is not going to be affected unless they are talking directly to them. I'm sure most people have heard a conversation that goes like this:

Debra: Isn't Emily gorgeous?

Emily's mother: She looks it doesn't she, but I can tell you, at home she's revolting. Not like her brother at this age – he was an angel.

What messages does Emily get about herself, her mother, her brother and her relationship to both of them? If Emily gets this message enough times, and at certain times in a young life, once is enough, she will start to fit into the role assigned to her by her mother and keep proving her mother right.

Our enormous emotional investment in our children sometimes gets in the way of us being good role models. It seems so unfair that my children always behave impeccably for other people and squabble and bicker with me. It frustrates and upsets me. Why should the person who loves them more than anyone else in the world get the worst of their behaviour? I find it quite difficult in these moments to stay calm and, frankly, grown-up. I am well aware that they are testing boundaries with me because they know that they are safe to do so, but in that moment I just don't like it.

Day-to-day stuff gets in the way too. We may be very busy with work or tired and therefore short-tempered. We may be worried about something and the children think we are worried about them. Children do not respond well to anxiety from a parent; it makes them feel very wobbly indeed.

We need to strive for consistency, even though it can sometimes feel like an uphill battle. Children need consistency in their lives to feel safe and emotionally secure. The world is a scary enough place without us adding to it at home.

One of the things that stop us from being a consistently good role model is our ability to manage our state. If we get frustrated or angry we are likely to behave in a way that is not useful either for us or our children.

The starting point is to become aware of what we are currently like as parents, good and bad, then to decide how we want to be as parents and equip ourselves to keep focused on that and maintain it.

Today's parent – Becoming aware

Remember the coaching framework.

Let's think about the **Present** – what is happening now. In any coaching, self-awareness is the first step. We need to know what we do now so that we can do more of what we like and less of what we don't like. We all have a sense of what we do and say but we rarely take time out to think about it and how it may affect the future of our children.

A friend of mine is usually in a hurry because she is usually late. She runs everywhere with her children running behind her attempting to keep up while she shouts: "Hurry up, hurry up, we're late again!" It wasn't until we had a conversation about how children are affected by our behaviour that she even realised that it was something she did almost all the time. Nor had she considered what negative messages her two children may be getting.

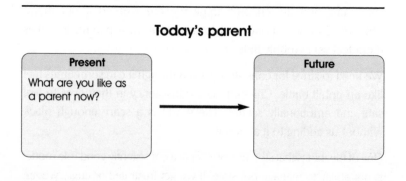

Today's parent

Present	Future
What are you like as a parent now?	

EXERCISE: TODAY'S PARENT

Take a few moments to think about yourself. Here are some questions to guide your thinking. Jot the answers down so that we can revisit some of them later. I asked a friend of mine, Ruth, to answer the questions and her answers are below.

1 What sort of role model are you now?

2 What behaviour do you see in your children that you realise they have learned directly from you?

3 What are you good at?*

4 What are you less good at?

5 What qualities do you have that you hope to pass on to your children?

6 What do your children admire about you?

7 What's important to you in your life?

8 What characteristics do you have that you would prefer not to pass on to your children?

9 What are you enthusiastic or passionate about?

10 If you are a working parent, how do you balance work and home?

11 What do you find easy about being a parent?

12 What do you find less easy?

13 What do you like about being a parent?

14 What do you dislike?

15 What do you do that you want to stop doing or do less?

---

* I asked my daughter what I was good at when she was four, and after much deliberation, her answer was, "Being cross." That was feedback for me.

Perhaps some of those questions were ones that you had not considered before.

What did you learn about yourself?

RUTH'S ANSWERS: TODAY'S PARENT

1   What sort of role model are you now?

- Strong (a bit fierce?!)
- Opinionated (wilful)
- Confident
- Happy
- Emotional

2   What behaviour do you see in your children that you realise they have learned directly from you?

- Strong opinions
- Happy and good natured
- Temper

3   What are you good at?

- Loving them – clearly, vocally, constantly

4   What are you less good at?

- Staying calm and keeping control
- Being uncritical
- Patience

5   What qualities do you have that you hope to pass on to your children?

- Courage
- Warmth
- Belief in themselves

6 What do your children admire about you?

- Cooking!
- Strength
- Competence – that I can deal with any situation

7 What's important to you in your life?

- Love
- Integrity
- Honesty
- Gin, wine and chocolate!

8 What characteristics do you have that you would prefer not to pass on to your children?

- Violent temper
- Tendency to criticise
- Impatience

9 What are you enthusiastic or passionate about?

- My family and my friends
- My home
- Books
- Cooking
- Art

10 If you are a working parent, how do you balance work and home?

N/A

11 What do you find easy about being a parent?

- Enjoying my children and having a laugh with them
- Advising
- Discipline

12 What do you find less easy?

- Staying calm
- Being patient

13 What do you like about being a parent?

- Talking to my children
- Physical contact with them
- Admiring them
- Constant change

14 What do you dislike?

- Chores, chores, chores
- Anxiety and anger I feel on their behalf
- Psychological battles

15 What do you do that you want to stop doing or do less of?

- Shouting
- Being horrid

16 What did you learn about yourself?

- I learned that I really like being a parent. Did I know that already? Now I'm convinced.

Now let's move to what we want – the **Future**.

Tomorrow's parent

Present		Future
	→	How would you like to be?

How do we get what we want?

People who get what they want consistently in their lives all have a similar strategy.

Firstly, they think about what they want, *not* what they *don't* want.

Secondly, they mentally rehearse having it already.

Thirdly, they think about the consequences of getting it, positive and negative, to themselves and those around them.

Fourthly, they make sure that they can take action themselves, and that someone else is not responsible for the action.

Let's take those in turn.

1 Think about what you want, not what you don't want.

Our minds can't imagine "not." "Not" only occurs in language, not in our internal representations. So if we tell ourselves not to do something, we are in fact instructing our mind to think of the very thing that we don't want.

Think for a minute about the following statements:

"I mustn't eat cake today."
"I don't want to start an argument with anyone."
"I must be careful not to slip."

As you read these statements, what images come to mind? Eating cake, having an argument and slipping over, probably! Whatever you imagine happening acts as an instruction to your unconscious mind to do it.

It is much more effective to give yourself the following instructions as alternatives to the above statements:

"I will eat healthy food today."
"I will be polite to everyone I meet."
"I will walk carefully."

With these statements, you will imagine what you *do* want, rather than what you *don't* want.

2 Mentally rehearse having what you want already.

We discovered that Thomas has an effective strategy for running races. He imagines himself running across the winning line *having already won the race*. In other words, he mentally rehearses the outcome. The more sensory rich your rehearsal, the more likely it is that you will achieve your outcome.

Ask yourself, how would I know if I had achieved the outcome? What would I see, hear and feel?

Mohammed Ali was excellent at mental rehearsal. He imagined he was in the future, fighting his next opponent and went through the whole fight in his mind again and again. He coined the phrase "creating future history" to describe this process.

3 Think about the consequences of getting what you want, both positive and negative, to yourself and those around you.

In other words, does what you want fit with who you are and what's important to you? Put yourself even further into the future and ask yourself, "What will happen if I get what I want? Will I lose anything that I have now? How will it impact on those around me and is it worth it?"

4 Make sure that you can take action yourself, and that someone else is not responsible for your action.

We are only responsible for our own behaviour. We cannot set an outcome for someone else to behave in a certain way and expect it to happen.

We have to look to ourselves first. What can *we* do differently that will make it more likely that the other person will behave differently towards us?

There are many parents who want their children to achieve specific things and a lot of their energy goes into their own personal outcome for their children. This can cause a great deal of family friction. Children can feel under pressure to please their parents and comply with their wishes, only to resent it later. Or they rebel against the parents' wishes earlier and the parents feel disappointment. Either way, wanting something for someone else is not useful and rarely works out.

As parents, of course we are going to have hopes and dreams for our children. What we can do is help them to find out who they are and what *they* want and support and guide them, so that we play a positive part in helping them to create the life they want to lead.

I remember seeing a well-known actor being interviewed by Michael Parkinson on his television chat show. His mother had recently died and he and his three equally talented and successful siblings had clearly been very close to her. Unprompted, he said that what had made his mother such a wonderful parent was that she always allowed, supported and encouraged them to be themselves and pursue their dreams. It made a huge impact on me. I felt that if my children said that about me, then I would have done a good job.

The easiest way to think about what we want is to pretend that we are in the future and we already have it. In this next exercise, assume that you became your version of the perfect parent, whatever that means to you.

If possible, find a quiet place where you can daydream for ten minutes and jot down some notes.

EXERCISE: TOMORROW'S PARENT

Imagine that it is 10, 15 or even 20 years from now and your children have left home. Perhaps they have children of their own. One day you overhear a conversation taking place between one of your grown up children and a friend of theirs. They are talking about you. Specifically, they are discussing what you were like as a parent; what your parenting did for them.

So you are now in the future listening to this conversation about you.

What do you *want* them to be saying about you?

Write down what they are saying about you – all the qualities they admired in you as they were growing up, how you treated them, what you believed in, what messages they got from you about themselves that helped make them the person they are today.

Now you have filled in the two boxes of the coaching framework. Compare your **Present** box with your **Future** box. What are the main differences?

RUTH'S ANSWERS: TOMORROW'S PARENT

This is the conversation Ruth hopes to be overhearing fifteen years from now.

"You could always talk to her about absolutely anything. She'd listen and tell you what she thought, but not tell me what I should think. It was important to her that we formed our own beliefs and opinions, and that we'd then have the courage to stick with them.

"She was always cuddling us – yuk! But it was nice really. She was such a laugh. We had some great parties, but I liked the times when it was just us, laughing.

"It was always good to have Mum in our corner – she'd fight anyone for us – the number of arguments she had with teachers . . . blimey!

"I'm amazed, actually, that she didn't chuck me out that time I shaved my head – or when you wrote her new car off. Do you remember? She went mad at that bloke who'd driven into you? Even though we all knew it was your fault really!

"I loved it when she turned 40. Do you remember how she dyed her hair purple and we all had to troop off to India?

"I just loved that she was always so passionate about us – even when she got really busy with work and stuff – she never stopped. Actually, I wish she'd phone a bit less – maybe just every few days – but you know Mum. Being a family is all about loving and sharing with all your heart – COME WHAT MAY!"

Making the changes

So how do we get from where we are now to where we want to be? How does Ruth make that dream a reality?

You have already made the first step by setting yourself a future "you" to focus on. As it is now in your conscious awareness it is more likely to happen. Why? Because in your mind, you have already rehearsed being the best parent you can be.

When you think of your future self, what emotions are attached to that? Positive ones I would guess. And the more time you spend in that positive emotional state, the more likely you are to do and say the things you want to your children.

Here is an exercise that keeps you focused on your future self. I have found it to work very well as a general exercise to help me to be the best I can be and a good reminder of the person I am trying to become!

EXERCISE : YOUR FUTURE SELF

Find a quiet place for this where you will not be disturbed. It will take about 10 to 15 minutes.

Make a list of the positive emotional states, qualities and skills that you already have and want to have as a parent. Use your list from the last exercise to guide you. Don't hold back – make a good long list.

Spend a few moments thinking about each item on your list, and what it's like for you when you are demonstrating that quality or feeling that emotion. If patience is on your list, for example, spend a few moments thinking about what it is like when you are being patient, and so on, until you have thought through each quality.

Imagine that you have a huge transparent beach ball in front of you that is big enough for you to step inside.

Now imagine that you are placing all the qualities, skills and emotions inside that beach ball. Really project them into the ball and fill it up with them.

Next, step inside your imaginary ball and feel all those qualities wash over you and breathe them in. Walk around in your imaginary beach ball for a few minutes. Notice how you are feeling as you walk round. What is different for you?

You may like to do this exercise every now and then to keep it fresh, adding to it or changing it as you wish.

Not only is this exercise very good for keeping you focused on your goals, it can help you to feel more able to handle difficult situations.

Every time you are in a situation that you might find difficult with your children, just imagine stepping into your giant beach ball.

Summary

- What are you like as a parent now? Use the questions on page 13 to guide you.

- What kind of a parent do you want to be? Use the exercise on page 20 to go into the future.

- Keep focused on your future self by practising the exercise on page 22.

3

Inside out and outside in

The process
of communication

In Chapter 1, I wrote that there are two main things that coaches need to understand, in order to coach effectively. The first is the coaching framework and the second is an understanding of the process of communication: how people process information, communicate, and organise their thoughts to create their unique internal world, and hence their unique view of the external world.

This chapter contains the explanation of that process.

Why is it important to understand it? It is important because it is the foundation upon which everything else in this book is built.

When you understand this process you will know:

- How we make sense of all the information around us.

- How we filter the information around us.

- How we create our thoughts.

- How our thoughts interact with our physiology to create emotions.

- How our emotions affect our behaviour.

- How most of this process happens unconsciously.

- How becoming aware of these processes gives us more choices in our behaviour.

In understanding this process you will also be able to help your child become aware of their processes to give them more choice in their responses and subsequent behaviour.

Our senses are bombarded with information. In every moment, millions upon millions of pieces in the form of sights, sounds, touch, taste and smell surround us. However, we can only pay attention, consciously, to approximately seven pieces of information at once, give or take two.* That is, we can pay attention to five pieces on a

* George A. Miller, *The Psychological Review*, 1956, Vol. 63, pp. 81–97.

bad day and nine on a good day. Do you remember playing the memory game as a child? Up to twenty random items were put on a tray and you had a few minutes to memorise them. It was rare that anyone remembered more than eight or nine items.

Also, consider how difficult it is to remember a telephone number if someone gives it to you in a way that is different to the way you normally group it. When the London telephone numbers were split into 020 7 and 020 8, people had differing views on how to group the numbers. Some people attached the new 7 or 8 to the 020 and some attached it to the next group of numbers. Once a telephone number gets beyond nine numbers, it becomes difficult to remember unless it breaks down easily into "chunks." And if someone presents you with a phone number in different chunks to yours, you have to stop and re-order them to remember or make sense of them.

So, we are bombarded with millions of pieces of information in every moment, and yet we can only consciously pay attention to a very small amount. What happens to all the rest? We simply have to **delete** it.

We also **distort** the information in order for it to make sense to us. Have you ever been absolutely sure that you saw your car keys in a certain place and that someone must have moved them, only to find out later that you left them somewhere entirely different? Have you ever been somewhere with a friend and realised afterwards that you had very different experiences. You have both been in the same place at the same time, and when you talk about it afterwards, you can't quite believe that you were!

There are some people who make a living out of their ability to distort reality: architects and artists are two examples.

Thirdly, we **generalise** the experience. Generalisation is the process by which we learn. Once, as a child, we have learned how to open a door, we don't have to re-learn how to open every new

The Process of Communication

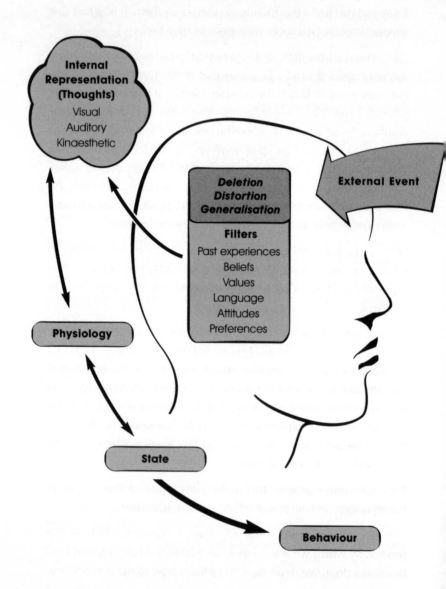

door we come across. We can generalise our experience of opening a few doors and apply it to new doors. Generalisation is also how we form beliefs. We may have one bad experience in a town and generalise that experience to believe that that town is dangerous.

So, all our experiences are subject to three internal processes: deletion, distortion and generalisation.

And if we do all these things, what exactly DO we pay attention to? It depends on the filters through which we view any experience. And what are filters? Our filters include our beliefs and values, memories, our preferences and interests. In short, all the coding of our past and present experience.

A few years ago, when we were about to get a new car, someone suggested a particular make to us that we had never even heard of. The very next day, we noticed loads of them. When I was pregnant for the first time, it seemed to me that everyone in our town was also pregnant! I had never seen so many pregnant women. That is an example of all three processes operating through my current experience of being pregnant myself.

All this filtering happens outside our conscious awareness.

To recap: we have an experience and we filter all the information through our filters which have been formed throughout our lives from our life experiences. These filters inform what we pay attention to in order to turn millions of pieces of information into a few. As a result of the filtering, we form our internal representation (thoughts) of the experience in our minds.

This **internal representation** is made up of images, sounds, feelings, tastes and smells. We have internal representations that are memories and we also create new ones for events that haven't happened yet, also known as our imagination.

Being able to access someone's internal representation is the key to understanding their experience. This enables us to either reinforce it where it is helping them achieve success or help them transform it, if it is limiting them in some way.

Here's an example of how this works:

Let's create an internal representation right now to demonstrate. Imagine you are going on a school trip with a class of children, it doesn't matter what age. What is the image that comes to mind? What thoughts go along with it? What sounds are associated with the image?

Firstly, your internal representation of the impending imaginary school trip will be informed by any previous experiences of school trips you have had, either as a child yourself, or as a parent helping out (your experience filters). It will also be filtered through your beliefs about school trips – do you think they are fun, or that it is a liability to take thirty children out on a day trip? And it will also be filtered through your beliefs about yourself in relation to the children. Do you think that children behave well or badly on school trips and will they pay attention to you or not?

So, your internal representation is made up of images, sounds, feelings and perhaps tastes and smells. These are your thoughts about the trip.

Physiology

These thoughts affect our demeanour, our physiology. If you are dreading the trip you will look different and hold yourself differently from someone who is excited about the trip.

Conversely, our physiology affects our thoughts too. If you stand tall and breathe deeply you are more likely to have positive thoughts about standing up in front of a group of people than if you hunch your shoulders and look at the floor.

Internal representation + Physiology = State

Your internal representation combined with your physiology is called your state or emotion.

Scenario 1

I am going on the school trip. My internal representation of the trip is this: I am imagining a group of happy children, smiling and laughing. They are really excited about the trip so they are noisy. I can hear their laughter in my mind. I am imagining myself learning new things with them and start to wonder what those things might be. I see myself with a small group of interested children discovering something new.

As I am having these thoughts, I start to smile and I get a warm feeling in my chest. I begin to feel excited about the trip.

Scenario 2

I am going on the school trip. My internal representation of the trip is this: I am thinking about a group of children who look like they are on the brink of being out of control. I am not sure that they will pay attention to me if I need to discipline them. I have an image of three boys running off and not being able to get them back. I am running all over the place trying to find them.

As I am having these thoughts, my brow furrows and my breathing becomes shallow. I begin to feel worried about the trip.

Your internal representation has an incredibly strong influence. If you have a "glass half empty" filter, you may be paying attention to what is not right in your life. Your internal representations may be of things going wrong. If you think about things constantly going wrong in your life, your physiology is likely to be downcast and you are likely to feel anxious, worried or even depressed for some of the time. If you spend time in that state, how likely is it that things will go right for you?

If you have a "glass half full" filter, you are more likely to pay attention to what is going right in your life. Your internal representations will be of things working out for you and that will result in a positive demeanour and a positive feeling. If you feel and act positively, it is more likely that things will go right in your life.

If you want to give yourself the best chance of achieving something, however small, it is really useful to imagine a picture of your achieving it. For example, if you have a meeting with a teacher to go to, imagine it going well. If you are going to meet a group of strangers, imagine them smiling at you and having a good time. If you want to go to the gym, imagine yourself working out really effectively. Picture yourself going round the supermarket in double quick time and remembering everything!

If you do this, you are more likely to get what you imagine as you are setting up your whole system to get it; you have the internal representation of getting it, your physiology will be positive and that will make you feel positive and motivated too. If you feel positive and motivated, you give yourself the best chance of behaving in a way that means you will achieve your outcome: your state affects your behaviour.

State and behaviour

The state that you experience as a result of your thoughts will affect your behaviour. Your state always affects your behaviour.

Back to the school trip: how are you likely to behave with the children if you are worried about the trip? How might you behave differently if you are excited and looking forward to it? You are more likely to notice good behaviour from the children if you are being positive yourself, because it is what you are paying attention to.

Being able to manage our state is a vital part of parenting. Helping our children to manage their state is an extremely useful skill for life.

A word about "conscious" and "unconscious"

There will be times when I refer to our conscious mind or our conscious awareness of something. What I mean by that is anything we are actively paying attention to in that moment. So the vast majority of the processing of information that I have been talking about in this chapter happens outside our conscious awareness. In other words it is taken care of by our unconscious mind, which is in charge of everything apart from the seven or so pieces of information that our conscious mind is dealing with.

A major part of a coach's role is to raise someone's awareness of their unconscious processes. The more aware we are, the more choices we have in our responses to situations.

In Chapter 2, you took some time to think about what you are like as a parent now and the type of parent you want to be. My experience so far is that the major obstacle I have had to overcome in order to get closer to being the parent I want to be is being able to manage my state effectively.

Let's look at ways to manage our state.

4

Getting into a right state

Managing our emotions

My experience of motherhood so far is that the main thing that stands between how I am now and my version of the mother I want to be, is the ease with which I lose my cool. I'm convinced that my children know exactly what irritates me and do it on purpose! Our children are testing us all the time, and it's tiring. They test us because they need to know what they can get away with and what they can't get away with. They need to know the boundaries of behaviour and they test their parents because it is safe for them to test their behaviour on someone who loves them.

As a result of being tested in this way, people who have never got into arguments in their lives and who avoid conflict at all cost, find that when they become parents, they start shouting like some sergeant major on the recruiting ground. We respond in ways that surprise us sometimes – I never would have imagined getting as angry as I do occasionally, before I became a mother.

One of the reasons we react in this way is the strong emotional attachment that we have to our children. It is much harder to stand back and think rationally when we are embroiled in an altercation with someone we care so much about.

Losing our cool or reacting in other negative ways to our children is not useful. Being able to manage our state more effectively when our children or situations trigger a negative state is enormously useful.

There are all sorts of things that children do that trigger these negative states in parents: tantrums when they are little, ignoring us, fighting with their siblings, generally behaving badly, not doing homework, leaving their clothes all over the floor and so on. These negative states are the ones that lead us to doing or saying something that, in more rational moments, we absolutely know is not going to resolve the problem in the long term. We are reacting in the moment, and that does not allow for rational thought.

Then our negative behaviour creates more problems. For example, if we shout at our children because they don't listen to us, they get used to it and begin to react only when we shout. They don't hear us when we speak at a normal volume. This causes even more frustration on our part. Of course, children aren't just reacting to us, they are learning from us in every moment, so they start to shout at each other at the slightest provocation.

How do we get into a state?

Just as you took some time to think about how you currently behave with your children, let's look in more detail at the states that you get into that you do not find useful and how you get into them.

In order to do that, first take a look at your answers to the **Present** questions on page 13 that you answered. What did you write down about what you do that you want to stop doing or do less often?

It might be shouting, as in the above example, saying things that you later regret, becoming tearful or something else.

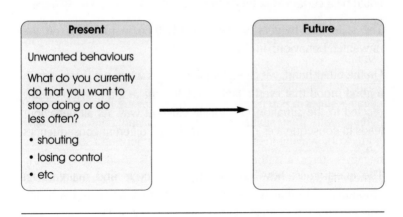

37

We need to become aware of what happens **before** we do those things. The more aware we are, the more control we have. If we are aware of the situations that cause us to behave in a way that we don't like, we can avoid some of them at least.

Remember: **state affects behaviour**.

How do we get into the negative state in the first place? Something sets us off, a **trigger**.

A trigger can be a situation, a place, something we see, something someone else says or does, a sound, taste or smell. Sometimes the trigger sets off a state so quickly that it seems to bypass the filtering and the internal representation that I explained in the last chapter. In these cases it all happens so fast that there are no conscious thoughts at all.

So the order of events is: **trigger, (internal representation), state, behaviour.**

We are going to pay attention to the trigger and the state for now.

In the example of shouting at the children, the trigger could be the children ignoring several requests for them to do something, or it could be a certain look they give you.

The state that triggers is anger which then in turn sets off the unwanted behaviour, in this case, shouting.

On the other hand, we can all think of times when we were in such a good mood that even a tantrum didn't shake it and we probably reacted to the situation in a totally different way. As all behaviour leads to consequences of some sort, we get different consequences too.

The question is: how do we break the cycle and maintain an emotional state that is useful to us and our relationship with the children? If we feel angry, how do we snap out of it?

First, let's look further at what specific things happen to trigger our negative states.

Being afraid of public speaking is a well-known, profound fear. What is it that triggers the fear in people? I work with a lot of people with this fear and the thing that sets it off is different for everybody. For some, it happens when someone asks them to speak, for some it hits them when they get into the room they are presenting in, and for one of my clients, it was the act of getting her "presenting" clothes out the night before that made her physically sick.

All our emotional states are triggered by something. Are there certain places that you go to which make you feel calm or relaxed? Are there certain smells that bring back memories that make you feel a particular way? For some people, the smell of newly cut grass reminds them of summer and makes them feel happy; the same smell for my sister reminds her of exam time and makes her feel anxious. Have you ever walked into a room that has set off memories, like visiting your first school many years later?

Music is another great example of a powerful trigger of moods. It's not for nothing that retro dance nights are so popular – they take us back and make us feel younger.

Here's something that happened to a friend and her daughter recently:

Jemma's story

Jemma, aged eight, and her mother, Susan, came home from school on their own one afternoon. Jemma's sisters were out for tea. Her mother was looking forward to spending the short time left at the end of the afternoon with her on her own. It was rare that they got to be on their own together and they usually had a lovely time. Jemma was very high-spirited that afternoon, in a very positive state, because she had spent the day on a school trip to a museum and had learned about Florence Nightingale, who she thought was amazing.

Susan seized the opportunity to suggest doing her homework. Oh, how quickly things can change! That was the end of the good mood.

First, Jemma suddenly decided that she was fed up that she wasn't out at a friend's for tea. Then, she decided that she was not going to do her homework. Susan made gentle attempts to persuade her. She tried to be patient and kept trying to coax her, but the longer Jemma ignored her, the more she could feel the tension building up inside her.

Susan started to get cross and reacted, perhaps unreasonably, by angrily packing away Jemma's homework for the night.

So far, the trigger was Jemma ignoring her, the state was frustration and the behaviour was packing away her homework. Of course, straight away Susan knew how ridiculous it was of her to pack away Jemma's homework, as it needed to be done. Here's how it continued:

Jemma reacted against her by immediately getting it out and starting it. But, as she was so cross by now, she didn't read the instructions and so spent the first five minutes answering questions incorrectly. This was followed by equally cross rubbing out.

Jemma also completely ignored all offers of help. As her first round of being angry was triggered by Jemima ignoring her, Susan's anger was ignited all over again except that it was anger mixed with frustration and then more anger directed at herself for losing her temper so easily. What a catalogue of events over something so small!

What was particularly frustrating for Susan was that she knew that if she had kept patient and light-hearted in the face of Jemma's mood, the afternoon would have been very different.

In this example, there are several rounds of trigger, state, behaviour. The triggers are obvious. Sometimes we just don't know what makes us feel a certain way. There is always *something* that sets it off; it's just that we don't realise what it is. So the first step in changing our behaviour is to become aware of the things that trigger our negative states.

Let's go on a hunt for some of your triggers. The easiest way to do it is to start with the situation, then think about the unwanted behaviour and then to work backwards to work out the state and finally the trigger.

EXERCISE: NEGATIVE STATES

1 Situation

Take a moment to think about the situations that you are in with your children where you get into moods that you don't like. These are the moods that then lead to you doing the things you don't want to do any more.

Where are you specifically? Is it in the morning before school? Are you helping to do homework? Trying to leave a friend's house after being for tea? In the car on the way home from school? Is it a meal time or bed time?

Make a list of all the situations and then choose **one** of these situations to think about as you answer the next questions.

2 State and behaviour

What happens in that particular situation? What is the state that you get into and the behaviour that you exhibit?

Tip: Sometimes it is easier to start with the behaviour and work backwards as in the following example.

Pam and Lucy

Pam has a daughter of nine, Lucy. Every morning Pam finds it a struggle to get her out of the house in time for school. Actually, they are rarely late, but Pam ends up feeling frazzled and has spent 40 minutes shouting at Lucy to hurry up. Pam is really fed up with doing this every morning; she goes to work irritable and she really wants to start the day more positively for all their sakes.

Situation	Each morning getting ready for school
State	[Unknown]
Behaviour	Shouting at her daughter and as a result feeling frazzled

In Pam's example, we don't know yet what state she is in just before she starts shouting – or what causes her to get into the state. We know what state she is in afterwards – frazzled!

Now we can ask Pam what state she was in *just before* she started shouting. Was she angry, frustrated, tired, or something else?

Here's what she told me about the situation. Her daughter is very easygoing and relaxed about life. Pam is very organised and busy. Each morning, Pam asks Lucy to get up at a certain time in order to be ready for school. Each morning Lucy gets up in her own time and gets dressed very slowly. Pam then thinks they are going to be late, which she hates, and she gets angry, stressed and agitated. The more agitated she becomes the more she shouts at Lucy, who still gets dressed at her own pace and manages to be ready just in time for school.

So now we have:

Situation   Each morning getting ready for school

State   Angry, stressed and agitated

Behaviour   Shouting at her daughter and as a result feeling frazzled

But what actually **triggered** Pam's stressed and agitated state?

It was *seeing Lucy getting ready at her own pace* and not Pam's pace, and her imagining that they were going to be late (internal representation) that set off Pam's state.

Negative states: Hunting the trigger

A question to help you become aware of how your states are triggered is:

What do you see or hear, just before you felt that way?

The trigger will be something that you look at, for example your watch, a certain expression that someone has, or something someone else is doing, or a sound that you hear, like a bell ringing or a certain tonality in someone's voice. In Pam's example, she saw Lucy getting dressed *slowly*.

If you can't immediately work it out, just keep curious and notice what happens next time you are in that situation.

Here's another example:

It's the children's bedtime. You ask them to go upstairs to get washed and ready for bed. They don't. You ask them again, nicely, and they plead for five more minutes which you agree to, on the basis that they will definitely go up then. They promise that they will, and carry on playing. Five minutes pass so you tell them that it is now time they went upstairs as they promised. They start asking for five more minutes again and when you say no, they go on and on giving you reasons why you should let them stay up later. Now, your patience just snaps and you feel really angry that they have broken their promise to do what you ask, again. You start shouting at them, and then, as you work yourself up into a frenzy, you start threatening all sorts of sanctions: no television (ever again!) and so on. You hurriedly get them into bed with them now becoming upset because you are still angry and you leave them to go to sleep without saying goodnight to them properly.

Of course, they don't go to sleep easily and you end up wondering how you could have handled the situation differently.

Let's break this example down.

Situation Bedtime

State Angry

Behaviour Shouting which leads to all the other behaviour

What was the trigger here?

It was the children breaking the promise and trying to get more time. That had become a trigger, because in this case it happened frequently.

Now work through your situations that you identified, separating out the trigger, the state and following behaviour. You may like to also identify the consequences of your behaviour as in the examples.

Here are some questions to guide your thinking:

- What is the situation that you find difficult?
- What happens?
- What do you do that you don't like? (Behaviour)
- How are you feeling just before you do the above behaviour? (State)
- What do you see or hear that causes you to feel that way? (Trigger)

What do you notice about your own examples? Is there a theme to them? What are the differences? Do you have many unwanted states or just one or two that keep recurring?

What have you learned about yourself from thinking about it in this way?

Another reason for knowing what specifically triggers unwanted states is that it is much easier to change the response to the trigger at that stage, in the next moment, than when you are feeling out of control. Imagine someone who has a panic attack when the person they are meeting doesn't turn up on time. The trigger turns out to be looking at their watch. It will be much more effective to change the person's thinking when they look at the watch, than to give them breathing exercises to do when they are in the middle of a full blown panic attack.

Negative states: Your role in creating them

Take another look at your examples:

What is your role in creating and recreating the scenarios that cause you problems?

Let's go back to Pam. Remember that she got very agitated about Lucy getting dressed at her own pace. Pam freely admits that she is frustrated by Lucy doing things her own way and not Pam's way. She is creating her own agitation by imagining that Lucy is going to make them late if she doesn't shout at her all morning. Does she know for sure that if she left Lucy to her own devices, they would be late? The answer is no, she does not know *for sure*.

How about the bedtime example? To what extent is that mother causing her own anger by thinking that her children (under seven) are going to keep their promise tonight in the face of overwhelming evidence that they will try for another few minutes' playing time? Of course they will. Not only are they young, they sometimes get away with it.

Positive states

Just as there are situations that you find difficult, let's put some balance into this by thinking about what you do currently that works well. There will be just as many times, and probably far more, when you have a lovely time with your children, when you all have a great time together and there are no cross words. It is equally useful to know what is going on when things are working just the way you want them to, so that you can do them more often.

Think about those times and situations and work them through in just the same way. Where are you? What's happening? How are you feeling? How are you communicating with the children? What is the response you are getting from them? And most importantly, what is it about the situation that causes you to be in a good and resourceful state? What happens in those situations when one of your children does something that would usually trigger a negative state in you?

For example, sometimes you may pick up the children from school or child minder and, having had such a good day, their bickering just passes you by, and you deal with it in a totally different way. What label would you give to a state like that? What states do you experience in your life now, which enable you to behave in just the way you want to with your children?

Make a list of the situations, states and behaviours that you currently enjoy and like in yourself. Use your original answers to guide you. Don't confine your answers to times with the children. Use other examples too. For example:

Situation   Taking them on a picnic

Trigger   Watching them having fun

State   Relaxed, peaceful, and happy

Behaviour   Responding to them in a calm tone, saying yes to their requests and having simple fun with them

Again, what do you notice about these answers? Are there any patterns? What is similar or different about the triggers?

Now you have a list of situations, triggers, states and behaviours that are positive and negative for you. If we were to put it into the coaching model and summarise it under headings it would look like this:

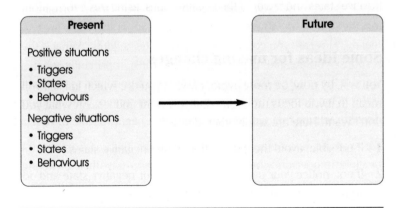

And here's a simple and incomplete example of what might be written in it:

Positive situations

Triggers   Watching them play nicely, planning a day out, hearing about something they've learned at school and are excited about, listening to certain music, running

States   Calm, playful, relaxed, proud, energised

Behaviours   Smiling and helpful, listening and making time, focused

Negative situations

Triggers   Being ignored, children not keeping promises, a certain look

States   Angry, resentful, frustrated

Behaviours   Shouting, getting upset, being unsupportive with homework

You are probably already thinking about how to create more of the positive states and fewer of the negative ones, using this information.

Some ideas for making changes

You will, by now, be more aware of what you do; which in itself will mean that you focus more on what you want and less on what you don't want. Here are some other ideas:

1   If possible, avoid the triggers that trigger negative states.

2   If not, notice your part in bringing on your negative state and do something different in the moment, however small.

3 Think of ways to recreate the situations that trigger the positive states; ask your children more questions about what they learned at school if that triggers a positive state in you.

4 Practise getting into positive states *before* a situation or time you find difficult. Listen to upbeat music before their bedtime, think of your favourite place in the world and imagine being there, before you do the school run.

5 Do the beach ball exercise in Chapter 2.

It is *much* more effective to change your state than try to *do* something differently. Remember, state affects behaviour; so if you change your state, you change your behaviour. There are other ideas on how to change state for you and your children in Chapter 8.

Finally, in this chapter, before we move on to how to coach your children, let's revisit the **Future** – what you want. Being very specific about what you want, particularly in relation to you and your states and subsequent behaviours, is a very effective way to create change.

EXERCISE: ADDING TO YOUR FUTURE SELF

Remember your beach ball? Have another look at the list of qualities, skills and states that you have and want to have to be the parent you want to be. Add any more that you missed previously.

Your beach ball list might include:

Happy

Relaxed

Calm

Playful

Kind

Understanding

Generous of spirit

Patient

Loving

Sense of humour

Curiosity

Fair

Consistent

Now imagine your beach ball with the future you inside it. Get a really good sense of watching yourself having all those qualities. Make it sparkly if you like, just for fun. Use your imagination and pile on the qualities.

What happens if I respond emotionally?

Isabella's story

Isabella is six and has a habit of losing control of her temper when she can't make a decision. On this particular day, it was about what to wear. Her family were going out for the day and her mother had given her three choices of clothes. She had previously found that this could be successful as she believed that it was important to give her children choices over small things so that they learned how to make decisions. Isabella started to lose her temper about the clothes. She didn't know which ones to choose and she got herself into such a state about it that everyone else in the family lost their patience pretty quickly. When Isabella gets into that state, it is difficult for her to get herself out of it, and she gets worse and worse, shutting herself into her room, shouting at her parents if they try to help and refusing to cooperate.

Given that this behaviour is unacceptable to her mother, her mother gets very cross, very quickly. Isabella usually behaves well but has a very wilful streak. Her parents have had some success in reducing the frequency of these tantrums with star charts and other behavioural techniques but her mother is absolutely sick of dealing with it and thinks that Isabella is too old for tantrums. She is so angry that Isabella is making them late, that she threatens to put her into the car in her underwear, and then tells her to get out of her sight until she calms down.

All of this escalates Isabella's tantrum and her mother's anger.

It is at this place in the story that Isabella's mother lost control of her responses; she started to say things that she would later regret. She told Isabella that she was glad to be going away on business so that she wouldn't have to see her, that she would speak to someone to see if they could have her for the summer so that she couldn't go on holiday with the family, and that she had had enough of her.

She told me that she knew in the moment that she shouldn't be saying those things, but she was just so angry that she felt she almost couldn't help herself. Her anger was a mixture of exasperation, embarrassment that her child was behaving in such a spoilt way, and anger at herself for handling the situation so badly. She said that her reaction was as if she was also a child reacting to her daughter.

Finally, they got out of the house, dressed and ready.

The fact is, however hard we try, there will still be times when we react emotionally rather than respond rationally. It may be because we are tired, worried or have just been pushed once too often that morning.

Experiences that are charged with emotion are filed as memories in their raw emotional state unless we are able to rationalise them and code them in a more conscious way. This is fine if the emotion is a positive one, and not fine if it is a negative one. This is the reason that talking things through helps us to feel less emotional because we start to make sense of the experience. It is not necessarily the experience that leaves emotional scars, but how the experience is dealt with or not dealt with afterwards.

Only fifty years ago it was thought that the best course of action for a child who lost a parent was to not include them in any grieving. I know people in their fifties who were not even given an explanation, and left to play on their own while all the adults gathered round to discuss the funeral in hushed tones. It was genuinely believed by some, that children wouldn't understand death and so it was better to say nothing at all. The experience of living through the loss for these adults is still extremely raw.

That approach is considered unthinkable now, as it is precisely the process of understanding – making sense of an event – that enables children to move through an experience and carry on with their lives. Now, it is more likely that children who suffer loss get support and counselling to help them make sense of the experience and move forward.

We probably all had experiences as a child, big or small, that are still raw memories. It may be something that now seems ridiculous or insignificant but it still remains as a difficult memory. Perhaps a friend's parent got angry with you for something that wasn't your fault, or a teacher showed you up in front of the class in a way that you didn't understand, or you were picked on by someone and no-one dealt with it. The point is, the memory is more likely to stay as a memory with emotions attached to it if you don't or can't make sense of the experience. Human beings are constantly trying to make meaning, so not understanding causes us stress.

When children can't make sense of a situation, they make up the meaning. They interpret situations for themselves to make it make sense. Sometimes their interpretations are the cause of distress for them. For example, it is very common for children to blame themselves when their parents' marriage breaks down.

It is very important therefore to help your child to understand and make meaningful interpretations of interactions with you and others, in a way that is useful for them.

Isabella's story continued...

Luckily, Isabella's mother realised that she needed to talk through what had happened that morning so that she could minimise the negative effect of her words. Here's what she did:

When she had calmed down she sat down with Isabella. She used the coaching model to guide her thinking. She told her that they needed to make sure that they didn't do that again to each other.

The Present

Isabella's mother took responsibility for her emotions and apologised for saying those things, which she did not mean. She explained that she was so angry that she felt like saying those things at the time. She explained what Isabella had done that had made her so angry. She also explained that it was her behaviour that she didn't like, NOT HER, so that Isabella would not get a negative message about her personality.

She helped Isabella understand and take responsibility for her bad behaviour. She told her that she would not be able to have friends round for two weeks and she would get the same punishment if she did it again.

Isabella apologised to her mother for behaving so badly and they both agreed that it must not happen again.

The Future

They started to think about what they wanted to happen in relation to getting dressed and going out.

In this chapter you've thought about the situations that you enjoy and the ones you like less; the states you get into, positive and negative and what triggers those states; and you have considered ideas for making changes. You have, perhaps, gained a better awareness of yourself and now it is time to turn your attention to your children.

5

What on earth is going on in there?

Understanding your child's thinking

I'm sure that you already know what your children are good at and less good at, what they like and dislike, what they enjoy at school and what they don't enjoy.

All these things are important. This chapter is concerned, not with what these are, but how your child organises their thinking *so that* they are good at whatever they are good at and like what they like. How are they thinking that influences them to behave in a certain way? What internal representations do they have of their experiences and how does knowing about them help us to help them?

Understanding our child's thinking processes is the key to:

- Understanding how they do what they do, both well and less well.
- Understanding how they make sense of the world around them.
- Understanding how they learn.
- Understanding how they create some of their problems.

In order to understand our child's processes we need to watch, listen and ask questions. A prerequisite for watching and listening effectively is being able to put aside your judgements.

In the words of one of the most inspirational teachers I know: "You must keep listening and observing all the time; don't form an opinion and then only listen to yourself."

As human beings the only way we can make sense of other people's experience is through our own experience. "I know what you mean" is a common and accepted expression. Except that more often than not we don't know what they mean. We can only guess.

Beware of assuming that you know what your child is experiencing. Keep asking until you are sure you fully understand. It is always better to assume that you don't know than to assume that you do.

Nail varnish story

*Hannah was playing with nail varnish one day when Thomas (then five) asked if he could put nail varnish on his toes too. Of course I said that that would be fine (pushing aside any judgment of boys and nail varnish that might have been creeping in!) and I helped him to do it. When we'd finished he said, "I think my friends might laugh at me." At this moment, imagining people laughing at me which I would not enjoy, I was tempted to say something like, "Well, you don't want that do you. You'd better take it off." Instead I **asked** him if that was OK if his friends laughed, to which he said no. I then asked him what he wanted to do next, and he said that he wanted to remove the nail varnish. So we did.*

In this example he was the one who decided if something was OK or not. At no time did I give him any interpretation of my own. Removing my own judgment of the situation meant that Thomas was in charge of his own thinking and he reached the solution to the problem quickly and easily on his own.

Let's think back to the communication process in Chapter 3. I used thinking about accompanying a school trip as an example of our internal thought processes and how they are related to our behaviour. Here's another example, this time with more detail added.

Think of the last time you went to the cinema or perhaps watched a film at home. When you were watching the film, all your senses were involved. You were looking at the film, hearing the soundtrack and experiencing the emotions that the director wanted you feel. You may also have been aware of other sights and sounds in the cinema; somebody blocking your view or shifting in their seat; people talking or eating popcorn. There will have been other feelings too. Was the seat comfortable or not? What was the temperature like in there? And you also may have been aware of smells and if you were eating, tastes.

Now, as you are thinking about it, you are recalling the memory of the experience. The memory probably has lots of information missing in comparison to the original experience. You will have remembered the things you were paying attention to at the time. Remember, that is what forms your internal representation of the original experience. If you saw the film with someone else, they will have a different internal representation or memory of the same experience.

So, our memory (internal representation) of any experience is formed according to what we pay attention to, and the things we pay attention to depend on our filters. We make meaning of our experiences according to many things including our beliefs, values, personal preferences and all our previous experiences – the basis of who we are. Therefore, this memory not only has information missing from it, it is also distorted.

When we talk about the trip to the cinema, our memory gets filtered again, through language. We don't tell people *everything* we can remember about the film, we tell them about the bits that we think will interest them, or a potted précis. In other words, we miss out and distort the experience still further.

You will remember that these internal representations inform our physiology, and also vice versa, (try having positive thoughts while doing the physiology of looking sad) and that our thoughts and physiology make up our state which affects our behaviour.

For now, it is this **internal representation** that we are interested in. I am calling it an internal representation and not a memory now because we also have internal representations of the future. We are constantly imagining what might happen, thinking about the trip to the supermarket, picking up the children from school, cooking their supper, thinking about what we will be doing at the weekend, worrying about certain things.

You may also remember that an internal representation can be made up of images, sounds, feelings, tastes and smells. Think about that last trip to the cinema again. What do you remember most: the images, the soundtrack or the emotions it elicited in you? If people ask me about the soundtrack in a film, I have to confess that I can't remember it – I simply don't notice it as much as the dialogue or the emotions I experienced. It is **how** you are thinking as well as **what** you are thinking which is important and interesting here.

We have already considered the impact of **what** we are thinking on our behaviour. We make pictures in our mind that cause us to feel anxious. For example, some of us start "imagining the worst" if someone we are meeting doesn't turn up on time. We may be making pictures of something going wrong and probably talking to ourselves in a negative way. Conversely, people who consistently get what they want are very good at picturing themselves having it already and give themselves encouraging messages that empower them.

Thinking differently

We all think in all senses. It is important that we remember this so that we are not tempted to put our children into pigeonholes that are not useful to them. You may notice that every time they tell you about a new experience, they tell you in a different way, in which case they have a very sensory rich internal world. Or, you may start to notice that your child demonstrates a particular preference.

Our son Thomas really pays attention to sounds. He loves music and he is always the one to ask, "What's that noise?" He gets easily distracted by noises that other people just don't notice. His sister Hannah pays attention to visual information above the other senses.

She has a very good visual memory so we always ask her where something is if we can't find it!

It is useful to understand how your child prefers to process information because:

1 You can communicate with them much more effectively.

2 They can maximise their ability to learn and overcome some learning challenges.

3 You can help them develop their other senses too.

There are three main modes of thinking:

1 Visual – thinking in pictures.

2 Auditory – thinking in sounds.

3 Kinaesthetic – thinking in feelings or describing actions.

We need to be in the coaching state of curiosity if we are going to become more aware of our children's preferences. So how do you determine what sense a child prefers to use, if indeed they have a preference?

What are we watching and listening for?

1 Their language.

2 Their eye movements.

3 What they pay attention to.

1 Listen to their language

How does your child describe their day at school? Do they talk about what things look like or sound like or do they tell you about the activities?

Visual language

If a child is using visual language, they will use words that visually describe something.

"A big tree fell down in Grandma and Grandpa's garden. It had lots of branches poking out and had a greenish trunk. It squashed the pink flowers in the flowerbed. We made a bonfire that was really tall with all the thin sticks and branches. The flames were bright orange and the smoke billowed out of the top."

Auditory language

When a child is describing something with auditory language, they will describe sounds and report speech.

"Grandpa cut the tree up with a chain saw. It was so noisy. It sounded like a motorbike. Grandma told us to stand a long way back to keep safe. When Grandpa lit the bonfire it really crackled."

Kinaesthetic language

When a child is describing something kinaesthetically, they will talk about what things they did and how they were feeling.

"I was helping Grandpa to pick up the sticks and logs. And then I helped Grandma rake the leaves. And I went to the mender's to fix Grandpa's electric saw. And I went in the wheelbarrow to the bonfire to put the logs on the bonfire. It was really fun and hard work."

2 Watch where they are looking when they are describing something- their eye movements

Our eye movements unlock our thoughts. The movement of our eyes sends an electrical impulse to our brain to access certain types of sensory-based information.

The information that you need about eye movements in order to do most of the things in this book successfully is:

- If your child is thinking in pictures, they will look up or straight out in front (as if looking into the middle distance) to see them.
- If they are thinking in sounds, describing perhaps a conversation that they had or a song that they heard, their gaze will be level, in line with their ears.
- If they are accessing feelings or talking to themselves, they will look down.

However, there are times when it is useful to have more specific information about eye movements; for example, if you want to help your children spell effectively.

Here's a diagram of someone's eye movements, as you look at them. Most people's eye movements are organised this way, although a minority are organised in a way that is a mirror image of this diagram so it is important that you check. If your child is left-handed they may be organised in the opposite way. Also, I have found that children's eye movements do not seem to settle down into regular patterns until they are about seven.

Eye movement diagram

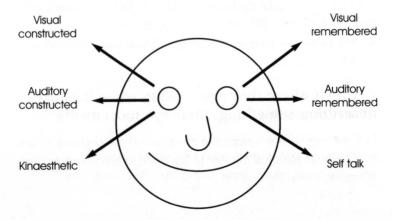

Visual constructed

Visual remembered

Auditory constructed

Auditory remembered

Kinaesthetic

Self talk

Try the game below with your children to see how their eye movements are organised. It is useful to do this because some of the things we are moving on to in the next few chapters require us to have this information. For example, if you want to help your child with spelling, you need to know which side of their visual field is the "memory" side.

EXERCISE: EYE MOVEMENT GAME

The answers are not important; just the eye movements.

Visual remembered

- What colour is your favourite toy?
- What was the brightest piece of clothing you wore recently?
- How many buttons has your Game Boy, TV, PlayStation, etc. got?
- What does your bedroom look like? (Ask questions about specifics in the room.)

Visual constructed

- Imagine a pink elephant with yellow stripes.
- What would a purple ice-cream look like covered in tomato ketchup?
- What would your Mum look like with green spiky hair?

Auditory remembered

- What sounds go with your favourite Game Boy game, etc.?
- What's your favourite song?
- Which hymn did you sing in assembly this morning?

Auditory constructed

- Make up a tune in your head.
- What would your voice sound like under water?
- What would your teacher sound like talking through a megaphone?

Self talk

- What do you say to yourself before a test?
- What do you say to yourself before a running race or a sports match?

Kinaesthetic

- What does it feel like when you've just run a race?
- What does it feel like when you read a poem in front of the rest of the school?
- What does it feel like when you put your toe in the sea?

At this stage just notice where they move their eyes when they are thinking about the answers. If you are not sure what your child is doing, just ask them, "What happened when I asked that question?" and keep curious. We need to get good at noticing eye movements to find out how our children organise their thoughts, so that we can help them overcome problems and be successful learners.

3 What do they pay attention to? Other clues

Children who have a visual preference

- Do they notice immediately if you are wearing something new or if you've moved the furniture around?
- They can probably tell you where your keys are when you've misplaced them.
- They like things explained in pictures.

Children who have an auditory preference

- They probably love music and notice noises that other people don't. They may need quiet surroundings to concentrate or find some places too noisy.

- They tell you about what people have told them.

Children who have a kinaesthetic preference

- They may be very physical, enjoy sport and are fidgety if they have to sit still for long.
- They possibly have difficulty learning certain things at school if they don't have an opportunity to *do* something during the learning.

What preferences do your children demonstrate? Do they think in pictures or sounds or do they prefer to act something out? Do they perhaps talk to themselves a lot?

Remember not to pigeonhole your children. We all use all of these systems. Labelling your child as "visual," "auditory" or "kinaesthetic" is not necessarily helpful. I worked with a teenager who was told that she doesn't visualise. Everybody visualises to some degree. This has caused her all sorts of problems. As a result of not paying attention to her visual information her ability to write creatively has suffered, because for her, she needed to use her imagination (visual) in order to generate ideas for writing.

Making the most of what you discover

Charlie's story

Vanessa has a five-year-old son, Charlie. She has found it difficult to persuade him to eat certain things, and she has a particularly difficult time persuading him to get into the bath. Charlie seems to be very musical, probably with perfect pitch. When she learned about preferences for certain senses, Vanessa had an insight that helped her speak to Charlie in a way that is very compelling for him.

Vanessa realised that Charlie prefers to use his auditory sense; he likes and is sensitive to sounds. It's what he pays most attention to. She planned to try some new ways of persuading Charlie to get into the bath and to eat his food. She bought food that made noises and also got some new noisy toys for the bath. When we next met, she was extremely excited about the difference this had made. She found that she only had to say to Charlie, "Hop into the bath and tell me what the water sounds like when you shake that toy," for him to jump in! The same thing happened with food. She was amazed by the positive reaction to: "Charlie, try that crunchy new vegetable and tell me what noise it makes when you chew it." New foods have become irresistible!

Joe's story

Joe is a very active boy, always on the go. He finds it hard to concentrate in class because he doesn't like sitting still.

His mother was having trouble getting him to sit down to do his homework. I talked to her about these preferences and she realised that he demonstrated a high kinaesthetic preference. They now approach homework in a totally different way.

He walks around while reading, he learns his spellings and times tables on the trampoline and his mother does as much as she can to engage him physically in his homework.

As a result, they both have more fun and Joe gets through his homework successfully.

Another very effective way of finding out how your child processes information is to ask them questions.

Dylan's story

Dylan is seven. His mother, Louise, always asks him, "How was school today?" His answer is usually "Fine." Imagine her surprise when she challenged him one day: "Dylan you never tell me what you've done at school," and got this answer: "Well, you don't ask the right questions!"

Louise was totally stumped by Dylan's reply and decided to put more thought into her questions.

The key thing with asking questions is to really consider what we are asking the child to think about. Let's take the example of trying to get information out of our children.

"How was school?" is much too vague for some children. In order to answer that question they have to run through the whole day very quickly in their mind. They do not have the capacity to choose one thing to evaluate. It is much more effective for you to choose one piece of the day to ask them about. If you know their preference in sensory-based thinking, start the questions in that sense.

For example, Louise knows that her daughter Morgana has a visual preference and so she starts the questions with, "Who was sitting next to you at story time?" Morgana gets a picture of the person next to her in order to answer the question. Louise has reconnected her with a specific experience and can now ask for other details that she is interested in hearing about. The first time she asked what story the teacher was telling, Morgana repeated the entire thing, reliving the experience.

If you specifically want to guide the answer to a particular sense, try some of the following questions.

Questions requiring a **visual** answer:

- Who did you see at school today?

- What was your teacher wearing today?
- What work is displayed in your classroom at the moment?

Questions requiring an **auditory** answer:

- What did you hear about today?
- What did the teacher tell you about/ talk about?
- What songs did you sing in music lessons?

Questions requiring a **kinaesthetic** answer:

- What did you do today?
- What games did you play at break time?

At any time we can also ask them directly. What pictures are you making in your head (visual), what are you listening to (auditory), what are you feeling (kinaesthetic)?

Here's an example of how these questions worked with Dylan:

Dylan

Dylan had come home from school saying that he had had a really good game of football. Normally, the conversation would have ended there. Louise, having thought about what questions would be effective, found herself taking him back to that experience. The result was that Dylan felt fantastic all over again and Louise felt like she had been at the match herself. This is how she did it:

Louise: *Dylan, can you get a picture in your mind of a really good bit of the football match when you were playing really well?*

Dylan: *Yes.*

Louise: *Can you tell me what's happening?*

Dylan: Well, I can see myself on the pitch with some of my friends in the team.

Louise: So tell me what's happening.

Dylan then went into great detail about what was happening in that moment as if he were commentating on the match. As he did that, Louise started to ask about the other senses:

Louise: As you look at those pictures, can you hear anything?

Dylan: Oh yes, I can! I can hear all the cheering and the shouting!

Louise: And how are you feeling now?

Dylan: I feel like I did when it happened – fantastic!

If we get this quality of information from our children, we can put it to good use.

Louise suggested to Dylan that any time he wanted to feel fantastic like that, he simply had to think of that piece of the football match. That memory will become a trigger for feeling fantastic that Dylan can access any time he likes. State affects behaviour!

Summary

- Put aside judgements.

- Be prepared to watch and listen.

- We have three main modes of thinking: visual, auditory and kinaesthetic.

- Notice your child's preferences by:
  - Listening to their language.
  - Watching their eye movements.
  - Paying attention to what they enjoy.

- Play the eye movement game.

- Use the language of your child's preference to engage them.

- Ask them questions in their preferred sense to connect them to the memories of their experiences.

6

It's the way you ask them

Asking great questions

If anyone ever wanted proof of the power and value of being able to ask questions, I would remind them of the story of Lindsay and her daughter Corinne from my introduction. You may remember that Corinne had spent four years suffering acute anxiety causing her to feel sick and sometimes be sick before school. Corinne finally stopped when she saw the school counsellor who discovered the cause of the problem through asking questions.

Her mother Lindsay said to me, "It's a shame that nothing I said to her made any difference." When I pointed out to her that usually it's not what we SAY that makes a difference, it's what we ASK she looked at me aghast. "Oh my God, you're right. I didn't know how to find out."

One of the key skills of coaching is being able to ask great questions and that's what this chapter is about.

The questions cover two areas:

1 How to get more information to increase understanding and avoid making assumptions.

2 How to unravel problems and challenge statements that limit them.

In the coaching model, these questions fit into the **Present.** In all the examples, in this chapter I will focus on the **Present** and then continue with the same examples in Chapter 10, moving into the **Future** and developing solutions.

Getting more information

Remember the communication process set out in Chapter 3: our internal representation of our experiences is formed by the processes of **deletion, distortion** and **generalisation.** When we tell someone else about an experience, we give a fraction of the information contained in our internal representation of that experience. In other words, we **delete, distort** and **generalise** still further.

For example:

Parent: How was school today?

Child: Fine.

Possible deleted information:

"I played football and we won. Charlie got injured during the game and had to go to the nurse. Lunch was horrible. We had soggy vegetables again. Charlotte's invited me to the cinema but I don't really want to go. Our history lesson was good. We did some cool stuff on gladiators and the teacher was really funny."

In every day conversation, we don't need the detail of someone else's internal representation – it would drive us mad. We have to make assumptions to have a normal conversation.

Sometimes, of course, it is perfectly OK to accept "fine" as an answer, but there are other times when it is extremely useful and/or important to find out what lies behind what they have said.

Pete and Laura

Pete and Laura were work colleagues and were on a management course to learn how to motivate their staff. First, they asked each other some questions to find out what motivated them. The question they asked each other was, "What's important to you at work?" They listed their answers which included things like: being respected, working as a team, praise, making a contribution, and enjoying their work.

Unsurprisingly there were some similarities in their answers – or so they thought! Next they were asked to find out what they both meant by those words. As they both had praise on their list, they thought they would start with that. Laura asked a simple and effective question: "What do you mean by praise?" As Pete answered the question, the colour drained from Laura's face. His exact words were, "I like to be praised from the rooftops, the more people that know, the better!"

At that moment, they realised that their versions of the word "praise" could not be more different. Laura liked to be praised by her manager, by letter, handed to her privately.

Imagine what would have happened if they had been responsible for giving praise to each other in the work place and hadn't asked each other the final question. Pete would have given public praise to Laura because he would have assumed that it was the same for her too. He would have been surprised to discover that she found that type of praise demotivating.

How often have *you* misunderstood someone because you simply haven't asked them what they mean? The basis of misunderstanding is thinking that your internal representation of a particular word or phrase is the same as someone else's. Have you ever shared a flat? Was your definition of "tidy" the same as your flatmate's?

EXERCISE: DIFFERENT PEOPLE, DIFFERENT MEANINGS

How do your versions of the following words compare with those of your husband/wife/partner?

Both answer the question, "What do you mean by ['fun' and the other words below]?" or "How would you know that something was [fun]?" and compare your answers.

Well-behaved

Tidy

Naughty

Discipline

Fun

Adventure

Sharing

Try asking the questions again when they answer until you have a really good idea what they mean.

Here's an example:

> **Me:** What do you mean by tidy?
>
> **Friend:** I like things to be put away.

This is still too vague so we ask the question again.

> **Me:** What do you mean you like things put away?
>
> **Friend:** I like totally clear surfaces.

Now I know. I also know they wouldn't want to live with me as my version is a bit different to theirs!

What differences did you discover?

If you want to understand what lies behind someone's words you need to do two things:

1 Use their words.

2 Ask them what they mean.

I want to play	What do you want to play?
School's great	What's great about school?
History's rubbish	What do you mean, history's rubbish?
Can we go on an adventure?	What sort of adventure would you like to go on?

Here's another example:

You might tell me that you like to go to the theatre. In your mind is WHAT YOU MEAN BY THAT STATEMENT, your internal representation. On the surface it looks obvious what you mean by that statement. Because it appears obvious, I will use my version of what I would mean by that statement to book tickets at the theatre.

I present you with some surprise theatre tickets for *Hamlet* in the West End of London. Oh dear. What you meant by "I like to go to the theatre" was that you like to go to the local theatre to see light-hearted plays or comedies.

So, if you want to know more, the most effective way is to ask "*What* do you like about going to the theatre?" When we ask the question, it is useful to think of it in terms of uncovering the information that the speaker deleted in the filtering process.

Let's consider this example again:

I like going to the theatre.

What information is deleted?

The following information, at the very least, is missing from that one small statement:

What I like about it, which theatre, when I like to go, how often and what kind of show I like.

So useful questions to ask to avoid assumptions if you were planning some tickets would be any of these:

- What do you like about going to the theatre?
- Which theatre do you like going to?
- When do you like going to the theatre?
- How often do you like to go to the theatre?
- What do you like to see at the theatre?

All of these questions are asking for information behind THAT ACTUAL STATEMENT, the internal representation. They all use the words of the statement within the question. Using their words keeps the speaker in their original thought. We make communication much more difficult if we change other people's words into our words when we are trying to understand them.

Consider this question, which is perfectly relevant to the theatre conversation:

What did you see when you last went to the theatre?

In order to answer that question, the person will have to access a totally new memory. There is nothing wrong with asking a question like that in conversation, of course. But I want to make clear that we need to be aware of how we direct the thinking of the other person with every question we ask.

If your intention is to fully understand the other person's current thoughts, then the quickest and most effective way to do it is to keep the questions phrased around their statement and use their exact words. As a result of using their exact words, your questions may sound a bit clunky to you, and may not be grammatically correct. It doesn't matter in this context. When we use someone else's exact words they feel heard and respected and they do not notice the grammar.

This takes practice. At first, ask yourself, "What am I asking them to think about with this question?", before you ask it.

Key points

- Think about what you are asking your child to think about before you ask the question.
- Avoid making assumptions by asking, "What do you mean by...?"
- Use their exact words in your questions to keep them associated with the same internal representation, even if it doesn't make grammatical sense.

2 Unravelling problems

The best coaches help people to solve their own problems, rather than offering solutions. They do this through asking them questions that help the individual unravel the problem, before asking questions to find out what they want. Once the person is clear about what they want, they tend to be able to come up with their own solutions.

Our tendency, particularly with our children, is to offer solutions, or comforting words, because we want to help. But we can't offer really effective help until we know how the problem is represented in their mind. Sometimes, we are at a loss to know what to do to help. Knowing how to ask incisive questions means that we can *always* help in some way. And as we continue to use this strategy, our children begin to learn to question their own problems.

Most problems are caused by thinking in a certain way and we hear about them, stated in language like this:

"I can't do maths."

"My friends don't want to play with me any more."

"I'm worried about my test."

"I don't want to go to Grandma's this weekend."

"I just don't like school anymore."

I ran a workshop once for some sales people where the purpose was for them to come up with some new processes for getting new business. At the end of the day, one of the group said, "This is all very well, but they won't let us do this." I immediately wanted to give her the reasons why she would be able to implement the changes, but I realised that asking some questions would be much more effective.

Toni: They won't let us do this.

Me: Who's "they"?

Toni: The Management.

Me: Who are "The Management" who won't let you do this?

Toni: [Rather sheepishly] Debbie.

Me: So Debbie won't let you do this. How do you know that Debbie won't let you do this?

Toni: I don't know. I guess I could ask her.

You will notice that all I was doing was asking her questions that uncovered more and more of her internal representation. To make sure that your questions do this, you need to keep being interested in what must be behind the statement in order for it to make sense to the individual and be causing them a problem in some way.

Let's consider some children's examples.

Thomas

Thomas came home from school one afternoon and told me that the girls in his class play on their own in the playground. He told me more and more details about their games and started to cry. I was rather puzzled as to what the problem was! How did the girls playing on their own affect *him* exactly? The questions going round in my head were: Did he want to play with them? Was he being left out? Were they being unkind to him in some way? However, these questions would not have been very effective.

Using the coaching model, I had to focus on the **Present** first. I needed to find out what internal representation he had that was making him upset.

There was obviously a relationship in his mind between them playing on their own and him being upset but it was certainly not obvious to me. I wondered whether he had made a connection that the right questions might just unravel. I asked a question that is extremely effective when it is not clear how what a child is saying affects *them*.

That is, "How is 'the girls playing on their own' a problem for *you*?"

Thomas: Well they play their own games.

I was still none the wiser so I asked it again!

Me: And how is their playing their own games a problem for *you*?"

What happened next surprised me even though I have witnessed it so many times before in so many contexts.

As Thomas thought about the answer, he realised that it wasn't a problem at all. It just disappeared. He quickly went from upset to puzzled to talking about something else!!

Laura's story

Laura is seven and is moving up to Year 3 at school. This is a big step because it means moving up into the junior department with the older children. She has been at the school for three years and has made some good friends in her class. The school, like many others, shuffles the children up so they get to be in a new class; some faces will be familiar to them and some less familiar.

When Laura learns of her new class, she is really upset. Her parents really try to find out why and gather that she is particularly concerned about not being with her close friend, Betty. They also guess that she is nervous about sharing a building with the bigger children, some of whom seem huge to her.

Her parents are at a loss as to what to do to help her to feel OK about next term. They tell her that she will make new friends; that her teacher is lovely; that the children aren't really that big, and she really doesn't have anything to worry about.

She is still upset.

At this point her parents do not actually know what she is thinking that is causing her to be upset. What does Laura imagine will happen as a result of her best friend, Betty, not being with her? Without knowing the content of what she is imagining, they are having to guess at solutions that they hope will reassure her.

They need to know the content of her internal representation before they can really help her.

So how do they find out? They have already asked her *what* is upsetting her which is a great way to start the questions. (Avoid asking "*Why* are you upset?" because children (and adults) tend to give answers that yield little information.)

Parents: What is upsetting you about your new class?
Laura: Betty won't be with me.

This is the moment that we usually start unwittingly to read our child's mind and try to help them with "Never mind, you'll make new friends," etc.

The statement "Betty won't be with me" is just the surface information under which lies the reason for Laura's upset, in the form of an internal representation of pictures, sounds and feelings.

Here are some questions that Laura's parents could have asked her that would give them more information about what she is doing to create her anxiety:

"What do you think will happen if Betty isn't with you?"

Or

"When you imagine that Betty isn't with you in the new class, what happens next?"

We can carry on asking "and then what happens?", until we get to the real problem. Here's what happened when they asked her:

Parents: What do you think will happen if Betty isn't there?
Laura: Well, I don't really know anyone.
Parents: And what happens when you don't really know anyone?
Laura: I won't have anyone to talk to when we are doing work.

So Laura is upset, not because of Betty, specifically, but because she thinks that she won't have anyone to talk to. Now her parents know what she needs.

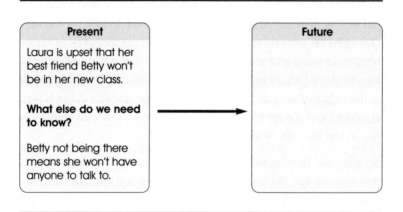

Present	Future
Laura is upset that her best friend Betty won't be in her new class. **What else do we need to know?** Betty not being there means she won't have anyone to talk to.	

Tom's story

Tom seems to lack confidence sometimes. He is six. He loves football and is desperate to join in with a large group of adults and children. His mum is there too playing in the group but despite that, he will not join in. She can see that he really wants to play and as time goes on he starts to cry and gets into state on the sidelines. His mum is very encouraging at first, making sure that he really does want to join in, coaxing him onto the pitch with kind words, asking him why he doesn't just run on to the pitch; all to no avail. As he gets more upset, she starts to get cross with him and when that doesn't work either she tells him to either get a grip of himself or go away because she doesn't want to watch him crying any more. Tom doesn't get to play football, his confidence stays low, and his mother is cross.

Tom's mother tried different approaches, none of which worked, and got cross with him because she didn't know what else to do and was so frustrated with the situation. Then she felt bad for ages afterwards.

In this example, Tom's mother's frustration was compounded by her lack of personal experience of what it is like to lack confidence. Our children sometimes have such different personalities to us, or behave in ways that we don't understand, that we simply cannot relate to their behaviour. If we can't understand them, we are limited in the help that we can give them. In this case, Tom's mother is very confident and always has been. She simply does not know what it is like to feel the way he does.

So what she needed to find out was how Tom was making himself feel unconfident. What was he doing that stopped him from running onto the pitch? No amount of coaxing, cajoling or shouting was going to get him on to that football pitch.

Pam: What was it that made you start feeling like this?

Tom: I saw a big boy from school get up to play.

Pam: What was it about the big boy getting up to play that caused you to feel like this?

Tom: I thought he might come up to me and get the ball off me.

Pam: What do you think might happen if he got the ball off you?

Tom: He would laugh at me.

Pam: And what would happen if he laughed at you?

Tom: I would cry and more people would laugh at me.

So now Pam knows how he is making himself so anxious that he can't play football.

At this point it is useful to repeat the whole thing back to them. Sometimes repeating it back makes the child see things in a different way.

Pam: So Tom, when you saw the big boy run on to the pitch, you imagined that he might come up to you and get the ball off you. And then you thought that he would laugh at you until you cried and other people would laugh at you.

Now that we know specifically how he is causing the anxiety that is preventing him from playing football, we have a much better chance of helping him to think differently. We have the piece that makes the difference.

The next step in our questioning is to challenge his internal reality.

Pam: Tom, how do you know that that big boy will get the ball off you in that way?

Tom: Well, he might.

Pam: And he might not.

Tom: I suppose so.

Pam: Tackling people is part of football, so what makes you think that people would laugh at you?

Tom: I don't know.

Pam has created doubt in Tom's mind now about what he thinks will happen. She can now start asking him about what he wants.

Present	Future
Tom is crying at the side of the football pitch and will not be persuaded to play.	
What else do we need to know?	
He imagines that the big boy on the pitch will get the ball off him and then laugh at him. Other people will also laugh and he will cry.	
After questioning he is beginning to doubt the above scenario.	

Susan and Isabella revisited

The description of the story in Chapter 2 was focusing on Susan and how she could minimise the effect of her losing control. Let's focus on how she can help Isabella. You may remember that Isabella gets frustrated and loses control of her temper sometimes. The specific example was a day when the family were going out and she refused to get dressed. What followed was a good example of Susan getting hooked into Isabella's behaviour and trying to get her to stop. It didn't work and it ended up with her mother losing control.

Susan does a good job of making sure that Isabella understands the consequences of her tantrums and the effect on other people and they have discussed what they want in the future – for Isabella to get dressed quickly when asked without having a tantrum.

So how come Isabella continues to have the tantrums about getting dressed?

Isabella's bad behaviour continues because Susan doesn't have the crucial missing piece of Isabella's internal strategy for getting into a state like that. She doesn't know what *causes* the tantrums.

So although Susan is sure about what she wants – Isabella to stop having tantrums and get dressed nicely – she doesn't know what Isabella needs in order to make her stop. Once she knows what causes her frustration, they can agree on the course of action.

Here's what happened when she found out:

Susan: What caused you to lose your temper in the first place?

Isabella: I didn't know what clothes to choose.

Susan: So you didn't know what clothes to choose?

Isabella: No.

Susan: How did you know that you didn't know what clothes to choose?

Isabella: I don't know I just didn't.

Susan: Were you making any pictures?

Isabella: No – nothing.

Susan: So your mind was blank?

Isabella: Yes.

Susan: And then what happened?

Isabella [getting frustrated]: I don't know – I didn't know what to choose.

What can we deduce from this exchange?

When Isabella knows she needs to make a decision, *she draws a blank*. She doesn't have an effective decision-making strategy. She has a blank space in her internal representation where a decision-making strategy should be.

Now Susan knows what she needs to do.

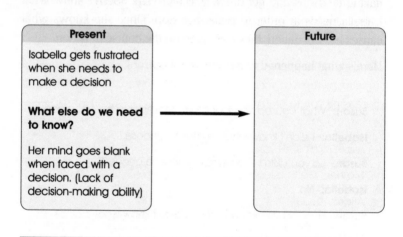

Present	Future
Isabella gets frustrated when she needs to make a decision	
What else do we need to know?	
Her mind goes blank when faced with a decision. (Lack of decision-making ability)	

This example might seem more complex than others, but bear with me; we will get to the solution later.

Alice's story

Alice is nearly six and is about to take her first tap dancing exam. She knows all the exercises and routines, has had extra lessons to help her prepare, has had lots of praise and encouragement from her teacher and even has the music at home to practise between lessons. Importantly, she has never been under any pressure to take tap lessons because she absolutely loves it and would go to lessons every day if she could.

Imagine her mother's surprise then when at bedtime five days before the exam, Alice started crying and said that she was worried about her exam.

Her mother's natural response was to comfort her and reassure her that she will be fine. That is a response that we all have, but it is not that effective in helping Alice to stop worrying. Telling someone not worry tends not to work because their internal representation of how they are causing the worry is too powerful.

Alice's mother knew that because she kept looking up, she must be making pictures so she asked her, "What are you thinking about that is causing you to worry?"

Alice: I can't tell you.

Mother: Can I guess?

Alice: Yes, OK.

Mother: Are you making pictures of something going wrong?

Alice: Yes. I think the examiner will be old and unfriendly.

Mother: So what does she look like in your head?

Alice: A witch.

Now that Alice's mother knew specifically what was causing Alice's anxiety about the exam, she had lots of choices of how to make Alice feel better. If she had tried to convince her that everything was going to be OK because she knew the routines and had been practising, in Alice's mind, she would still be performing in front of a witch!

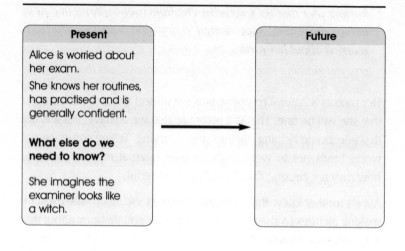

Alice's mother's question, "What are you thinking about that is causing you to worry?" is an excellent question to find out what is happening now. As with this example, we quite often have to coax the answer from our child in order to move on. Over time, they will get used to the questions and be more aware of their own processes. When they volunteer information like this, you have made significant progress. You have helped them gain personal awareness that will always help them deal with problems in the future.

Tara's story

We were lucky enough to go on holiday with some great friends of ours last summer. At the time of the holiday, their three daughters, Ella, Tara and Martha, were six, just five and two years old, respectively. The girls and our two children are all great friends so it was very exciting for us all.

One of the most exciting things for all the children was being able to swim every day in the villa's swimming pool. This was the first year that the four older children were fairly confident in the water. This meant that they could spend what seemed like hours every day in the water having a wonderful time. They enjoyed jumping in and inventing elaborate games that got more daring by the day. All of them made fantastic progress in confidence and in their ability to swim. They particularly enjoyed jumping in off the side and pretending to be mermaids and dolphins. We had one sticking point. Tara, just five, would not jump in and would not take her armbands off, despite having made good progress in swimming lessons without them. She was getting more and more frustrated as she watched the other three jumping in and having such a great time. Her mother, Claire, and I could see how it was upsetting her and the other three children really wanted her to join in.

Claire was exasperated that no amount of coaxing and offers of help were working, and she was concerned that Tara was missing out on the fun that her friends were having.

I wondered if there was anything I could do to help. Considering how much Tara wanted to play with the others, I realised there must be something pretty powerful going on in her mind that was stopping her from jumping in.

Tara knows me very well so, with Claire's permission, I asked Tara a few questions to find out what she was thinking. The result was absolutely amazing: after only a few questions and one suggestion Tara jumped in on her own before I even had time to get into the water to catch her!

So what were the questions? First, I asked her if she *wanted* to jump in like her friends. I was pretty certain that she did, but as I prefer not to assume, I wanted to hear it from her. She said that she really wanted to, so now my job was to find out how she was making herself so anxious.

Me: What do you think might happen if you do jump in?

Tara: Well, I think I might drown.

Tara actually had an image of herself drowning as a result of jumping in. No wonder she wouldn't do it. In fact, it is a very sensible decision not to jump in if you think you are going to drown.

Finding out what was stopping Tara from jumping was the key to finding out why encouragement and coaxing wasn't working.

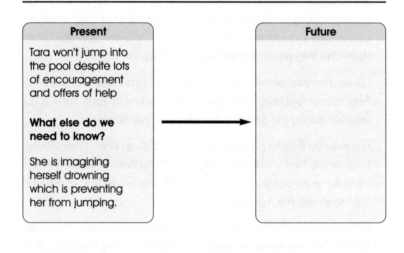

Present	Future
Tara won't jump into the pool despite lots of encouragement and offers of help **What else do we need to know?** She is imagining herself drowning which is preventing her from jumping.	

Finally, imagine if your child comes home one day from school and says that no-one likes her. Children are very quick to make sweeping statements about themselves in this way and we need to prevent this kind of statement becoming embedded as a belief. My knee-jerk reaction to this kind of statement would be to immediately say, "Nonsense!" partly as an emotional reaction to them even thinking that way.

Just like everything else, we need to find out her internal representation for that statement. The easiest way to do that is to ask, "How do you know?" or "What do you mean by that?"

Remember that our outcome is to find out what she is thinking, not to convince her that she is wrong. At this time, when she tells you that no-one likes her, she is telling you what is real for her. Once we find out her internal reality, we are in a position to encourage her to think differently.

> **Jennifer:** No-one likes me any more.
>
> **Mother:** How do you know that no-one likes you anymore?
>
> **Jennifer:** Well, Mary and Elizabeth didn't include me in their game today.
>
> **Mother:** So how does Mary and Elizabeth not including you in their game today mean that *no-one* likes you any more?

In this example, Jennifer had attached the experience of Mary and Elizabeth not including her in their game to a meaning of no-one liking her any more.

It is in questioning this attachment that we will have the most impact. If we manage to break the relationship between Mary and Elizabeth not playing with her and her thinking that means that no-one likes her any more, then the problem ceases to exist in its original form.

Summary

- Think about what you are asking your child to think about before you ask the question.

- Avoid making assumptions by asking, "What do you mean by...?"

- Use their exact words in your questions to keep them in the same internal representation.

USEFUL QUESTIONS FOR PROBLEMS

1 What do you mean by ... ?

This question gives you an understanding of what lies behind the surface of their words. It is good for clarification and avoiding assumptions.

Child: I want to go on an adventure.
Parent: What do you mean by an adventure?

2 What would you be doing if ... ?

This is an alternative to the above question and can be used to clarify someone's meaning too.

Child: I just want to have some fun.
Parent: What would be doing if you were having fun?

3 How do you know that ... ?

We cause ourselves a lot of problems by guessing what someone else is thinking. We quite often make statements like, "I know so-and-so will be upset if I don't tell them." We think that we know the mind of the other person.

This question challenges the person to think about the evidence for their stated problem.

Child: Sophie doesn't like me any more.
Parent: How do you know that Sophie doesn't like you any more?

4 How is [x] a problem for you?

If we state a problem as if it doesn't belong to us, it is difficult to solve. This question reconnects the problem with the person and as a result, the problem sometimes goes away on its own.

Child: The girls always play on their own in the playground.
Parent: How is that a problem for you?

5 What caused you to start feeling like this?

If your child is upset it is more useful to ask what caused it than ask why they are upset.

Parent: What caused you to get upset?

Or

Parent: What happened just before you got upset?

6 How did [scenario] cause you to feel like this?

This is a follow-up question to the one above when you need more clarity.

Parent: What caused you to get upset?

Child: Sally was playing with Tom at play time.

Parent: How did Sally playing with Tom at play time cause you to get upset?

7 How does [x] mean [y]?

This question challenges the connection between one statement and another.

Parent: What caused you to get upset?

Child: Sally was playing with Tom at play time.

Parent: How did Sally playing with Tom at play time cause you to get upset?

Child: It means I'm not her friend anymore.

Parent: How does Sally playing with Tom at play time mean you're not her friend anymore?

Keep listening and keep practising these questions. The more you practise the easier it will become and the more you will notice.

7

It's the way you tell them

The power of language

It is, of course, not just questions that direct our thinking, but statements too. What you say is as important as what you do. In my work as a coach, I sometimes find myself helping my clients get over the messages they were given as children, so that they feel more positively about themselves.

In this chapter I will examine how our language impacts on our children's thoughts, actions and beliefs about themselves and others. This chapter explains the importance of positive language in all aspects of communication and how easily we can install limiting beliefs in children by the use of careless language. More specifically, it will cover how to:

- Use language that helps them to form useful beliefs about themselves and others.
- Give instructions to get what you want.
- Build effective relationships with them.
- Use language they understand.
- Avoid "toxic" language.

Mind your language – it matters

Using positive language is an effective way to get what you want and grow happy, confident children. It is not about simply putting a sugar coating on things.

Negatively phrased language is present all around us, even when it's well-meaning. "Stop fighting. Stop shouting. Don't run into the road. Be careful you don't fall. Don't argue with your sister."

Remember from Chapter 2 that our minds cannot process "not." Negation only exists in language, not in experience. A child that is told, "Don't run into the road" has to go through a sophisticated process in order to make sense of it. The child will immediately imagine running into the road and then have to tell himself he mustn't do that. He still has an internal representation of running into the road that means he is still unconsciously paying attention to running into the road rather than staying on the pavement.

Consider this:

> We can't not think about what we don't want to think about,
> until we have thought about it first.

Our intention when telling our children not to run into the road is to keep them safe. A much better way to keep them safe is to tell them what we *do* want them to do: "Stay on the pavement." As soon as we give them an instruction like this, they imagine staying on the pavement. Running into the road doesn't even enter into their thoughts.

As children get older they may replace the initial internal representation with a new one of staying on the pavement, but that is an even more sophisticated process, and one that we certainly cannot guarantee that they will be able to go through.

Putting language into positively phrased instructions, that is what you *do* want children to do, makes it much easier for them to comply.

The differences in the statements below are powerful. Imagine being given these instructions yourself as you read them.

Don't look at anyone else's work	vs.	Stay focused on your work
No fighting in the playground	vs.	Play nicely with your friends
Stop messing around	vs.	Sit down quietly
Nobody is to run off	vs.	Everyone stay together
Don't forget your homework	vs.	Remember your homework

How many school rules are phrased in terms of what we don't want children to do?

How often do you hear yourself saying, "I have just asked you not to do that, so how come you went ahead and did it?" Now you know the answer! We plant ideas in the minds of our children, unwittingly, with the use of negatively phrased language.

The children's writer Roald Dahl makes this clear in the following passage from *George's Marvellous Medicine*:

> *"I'm going shopping in the village," George's mother said to George on Saturday morning. "So be a good boy and don't get up to mischief."*
>
> *This was a silly thing to say to a small boy at any time. It immediately made him wonder what sort of mischief he might get up to.*

Of course it did. George had to think about mischief and make pictures of what that means to him, in order to understand his mother's request. By the time he had flashed through some of those ideas, he was quite in the humour for making mischief!

The key is to always think, "What do I want the child to think about?"

Fiona's story

"I have had three children round for tea this afternoon and an interesting 'language moment'. There were two eight year olds and one six year old. They began to play with the outside tap and the watering can. Needless to say I foresaw sodden bodies and a cross parent taking two wet children home in the car. 'Don't get wet' I said, and basically got ignored. None of them even looked up and they carried on as if I had said nothing.

I instantly realised that I had used the dreaded 'don't'. I waited a few seconds and this time I said, 'Guys: STAY DRY', deliberately stressing the statement. Each one looked directly at me and engaged with me. They listened and they heard.

'Shall we just go and play inside?' suggested one of them, and dropped the watering can on the ground!!

I can't believe it!"

How many times do you hear parents say, "I have asked her again and again not to do that and she just keeps doing it."? Tim and I catch ourselves doing this quite often.

Hannah on a bicycle: "Hannah don't go too fast round that corner." Oops! What I meant to say was: "Hannah, slow down as you get to the corner."

"Thomas, don't get in her way!" Oops! "Thomas, stand well clear."

The difference is clear. When Thomas was given the instruction, "Don't get in her way!" he didn't move. As soon as Tim changed it to, "Thomas, stand well clear of Hannah," he moved.

When we rephrase our instructions in a way that states what we want them to imagine, children comply much more easily.

EXERCISE: USING POSITIVE LANGUAGE

Over the next week listen to your language and the language of those around you as you give instructions to your children. If you hear someone else give a negatively phrased instruction, notice what effect it has and how many times the instruction has to be repeated in order for it to have the desired effect.

If you catch yourself giving negatively phrased instructions, stop yourself and rephrase them.

BEWARE! "Toxic" language

Sometimes the language we use is not just confusing, it can be damaging. How about this for an example of confusing language:

Elizabeth's story

Alice took her niece, Elizabeth, to school on the first day of a new term. Elizabeth was seven at the time and considered very bright. The class was to be streamed into two groups for the first time and Elizabeth was in the top stream. When they arrived in the classroom, there were two large tables that had signs above them. One read, "EASY TABLE" and one read "DIFFICULT TABLE."

Which one should Elizabeth sit at? The EASY table because she finds the work easy or the DIFFICULT table because she will be given more difficult work than the other group?

Alice found out that, as she suspected, Elizabeth was to sit at the table labelled DIFFICULT. What also didn't surprise her was that Elizabeth wasn't particularly pleased at having to sit there. She said that she didn't want to do difficult work because she wasn't used to finding the work difficult. She was confused because she finds the work easy normally so why would she go to the DIFFICULT table. She thought she should be sitting at the EASY table.

Even thinking about this use of language makes my brain feel like a lump of cauliflower! Not only is this labelling of the tables incredibly confusing, what messages were the children being given and what conclusions were they going to make about their own abilities?

Children are very literal about meaning and they make meaning out of everything. They will make meaning out of confusion to make it make sense for them. What meanings will those children in that classroom make?

We can only guess, but some of them might be:

- Being clever means finding work difficult.
- Why do I find the work difficult when it says EASY table? – I must be stupid.
- Why do I have to do difficult work just because I do it quickly? I'll slow down so I can go to the easy table.

I find it absolutely incredible that whoever put up those signs didn't think it through. All people in authority are in a position where their words can have a major impact on a young life; parents, teachers, doctors, specialists. As adults we *must* consider the potential consequences of the messages we give our children.

Here are some examples of statements that should carry a **health warning:**

You'll never be any good at art.

Your sister got the looks and you got the brains.

You'll never be a singer.

You are the class clown.

Girls don't really need to get a good education.

You're just like me – the black sheep of the family.

You don't visualise.

It's just the way you are.

We are no good at maths in this family.

The impact of statements like these on a child largely depends on the child's personality. We have all heard stories of people who were given negative messages about themselves who then spent their lives disproving the statement and ended up being very successful.

We met someone at a conference who owned a large business. He told us that the reason he was so successful was because of a comment his headmaster had made to him when he was about ten.

He had stopped to hold the door open for him and some teachers one morning. As the headmaster walked through the door, he turned to the boy and said, "That's just about all you'll ever be good for, holding doors open for other people." In that moment, he knew he had to prove him wrong.

That story could have had a very different ending. We cannot trust to luck that slighting comments will turn out OK in the end.

On the other hand, my father was given the message, "It doesn't matter how you do at school, there's a job waiting for you." Some people might think that that wasn't a negative message. It ended up having a negative impact on him because he really didn't pay any attention to how he did at school. He now wonders how his working life might have turned out differently if he had been encouraged to do well despite having a job lined up at the end.

Language like the examples above contributes to children forming beliefs about themselves. So does positive language. So let's be conscious about using positive language so that we do our best to help our children have useful beliefs about life, themselves and others.

What are beliefs?

Beliefs are thoughts that form our reality. They are thoughts that we consider to be true. Remember the communication process in Chapter 3. Beliefs are filters. Our experiences are filtered through our beliefs; we pay attention to information that supports our beliefs. As our beliefs act as filters, our thoughts (internal representations) are affected by them, and so they influence our physiology, state and behaviour. Our beliefs have a major impact on our life.

Our beliefs remain remarkably consistent over time because we are constantly, but unconsciously, looking for evidence that they are true for us.

The Belief Cycle demonstrates the impact that our beliefs have on our behaviour.

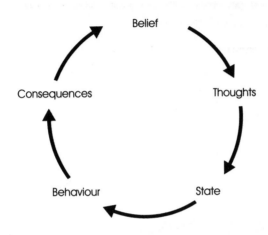

For example, I have worked with a lot of adults who believe that they are no good at standing up in front of a group of people to present something.

Here's what is likely to happen when they are asked to make a presentation.

Belief

I am no good at presenting.

Thoughts

Oh no. I wish someone else could do this for me. I hate it. It's going to be awful.

State

Nervous, anxious and butterflies in stomach.

Behaviour

If you are nervous while presenting, you are likely to avoid eye contact, speak quickly and haltingly, breathe rapidly, and display a lack of engagement with your audience and lack of confidence in your message.

Consequences

The audience will be disengaged and there will be a perception of you as lacking confidence and lacking conviction in your message.

As a result, your belief that you are no good at presenting will be reinforced.

The consequences of our behaviour are in line with our beliefs, proving to us that we were right to have that belief in the first place.

Here are some further examples:

I know someone who believes that anyone in the service industry is out to rip him off. At some point of course that must have happened for him to form that belief in the first place, or he may have learned it from a parent or adult who was significant to him.

However, continuing to have those thoughts about everybody he meets in the service industry causes him lots of problems. Whenever he has an interaction with someone in a shop, restaurant, garage or anywhere else, he is already thinking badly of the person in front of him. His whole mind and body are set up to protect him from being ripped off. So guess what happens? He gives out lots of unconscious signals about not trusting them and they respond by doing the absolute minimum for him in terms of service. At worst, they find themselves in a position where they *feel like ripping him off*.

If you believe you are a bad mother you will pay attention to examples that prove to yourself that you are, and dismiss examples that show you to be a good mother.

Some people's beliefs are so strongly entrenched, that other people get sucked into them. I know someone who absolutely believes that other people will not do what she wants them to do for her. All her attention goes into thinking that they won't deliver their promises. Because of her behaviour, I found myself in a position recently with her where I felt like not doing what I had agreed to do for her!

Whatever you believe, either positively or negatively, you tend to be right.

EXERCISE: A PARENT'S BELIEFS

- What are your beliefs about yourself as a parent?
- What are your beliefs about your children?
- What evidence do you have to back them up?
- Are they useful and empowering or do they limit you in some way?

Listen out for your children's beliefs about themselves and others so that you can help them to form beliefs that will become useful and empowering for them as adults.

How do we get to believe what we believe?

Our brain is a phenomenally powerful organ, which we are still only beginning to understand. It has been well documented since the 1950s that the brain records every single event in our lives. That of course includes verbal messages that we hear around us, even when we are not actively paying attention, which go straight to our unconscious mind.

Our messages to our children are a form of hypnosis. If they hear something often enough, consciously or unconsciously, it becomes true for them. At the beginning of Chapter 2, I used this example of parents who talk about their children negatively within their earshot as if the child is not going to be affected:

Debra: Isn't Emily gorgeous?

Emily's mother: She looks it doesn't she, but I can tell you, at home she's revolting. Not like her brother at this age – he was an angel.

I asked in that chapter what messages Emily gets about herself, her mother, her brother and her relationship to both of them from this flippant statement. If Emily gets this message regularly from her mother, she will start to fit into the role assigned to her. What impact will that have on her beliefs about herself, and subsequent behaviour as she grows up I wonder? Sometimes, a child only needs to hear something once for it to become a belief.

Consider the following extreme but sadly true example:

George's story

This happened in the 1930s to a friend of my grandfather. George was seven and an only child. He was devoted to his father and hung on his every word. They enjoyed each other's company and had a close relationship.

One day his father said to him: "Come on, George, you go up to the top of the stairs and jump and I will catch you." George was a bit concerned, but liked jumping down the stairs so when his father kept encouraging him and promised that he would be there at the bottom, he agreed.

"Come on, George, I'm here," his father kept saying.

George finally plucked up courage and jumped.

As he jumped, his father moved to one side and George landed in a heap at the bottom of the stairs. Confused and somewhat bruised, George looked up at his father.

"Let that be a lesson to you George. **Never trust anyone.** *"*

Poor little George. What an extreme way to form a belief about other people. What happened to George? He grew up not trusting anyone. He was always on the look out for people he couldn't trust and got involved with more untrustworthy people than any of his colleagues. Beliefs are self-perpetuating – we put a great deal of energy into proving to ourselves that we are right.

Sarah's story

Sarah is 14. She came to see me because she had some difficulties at school that were a bit unusual. There were two areas that were causing the teachers and her parents concern:

1 She was able to solve quite complex maths problems easily, and yet consistently got easy maths problems wrong.

2 Her English, which used to be excellent, has slipped in the last few years.

Let's start with the maths. She was told when she was about seven that she was no good at maths. She certainly found it difficult and formed a belief, based on her experience, that "maths is difficult." She had so many problems with maths that she started having extra lessons when she got to secondary school that took her back to basics. She worked very hard on improving her maths and it all started to click into place with excellent results.

So how come she manages to solve the difficult problems now and not the simple ones? Here's how: she is so entrenched in the belief that "maths is difficult" that when she looks at a "difficult" problem she is OK with that – it confirms her belief. She has caught up with her maths skills through her extra lessons and diligently works out the problem.

However, when she looks at a problem that she considers simple, she says to herself, "It can't be that easy." She then thinks, "If it can't be that easy, the answer that looks obvious can't be the right answer," and she proceeds to try to get another answer, which turns out to be wrong. That's how powerful beliefs are.

I noticed a pattern in the things she was telling me. She is a very bright student – this has never been in question. However, she has been told time and time again that she "has problems." As a result of this, whenever she is faced, in any subject, with a simple question that has an obvious answer she finds it impossible to accept the simplicity of it and assumes that because she "has problems" the answer has to be complex. Then she can't answer it because she has no idea what the alternative answer might be. The fact is – there is no other answer, it really is a simple question.

Believe it or not, all I had to do was to make this positive suggestion to her: "The next time you look at something that seems easy, just say to yourself, 'Great, this *is* simple!'" This suggestion made perfect sense to her. It resulted in her realisation that she had unknowingly been sabotaging her schoolwork. Simply knowing this enabled her to stop doing it and believe that when she thinks something's simple, she's right.

There was something similar happening with her English. She had been diagnosed a few years ago with a form of dyslexia despite not having any trouble with reading, writing or spelling. During the diagnosis she was told that she "doesn't visualise." She completely accepted that diagnosis from the expert, as most of us would, and as a result believed that she didn't visualise. Everybody visualises to a *certain* extent, even if they are unaware of it.

Believing that you don't visualise works as an instruction to your unconscious mind not pay attention to your mental images. It is essential to pay attention to those images for all sorts of activities like comprehension and creative writing.

Not paying attention to these images, even at an unconscious level, meant that Sarah's writing ability had declined. During our meeting, I noticed her visualising a lot, and pointed it out to her. She was amazed by this piece of self-awareness. I suggested that she spent some time allowing herself to daydream and notice images as they come to mind. She was very excited at the prospect.

So children form beliefs about themselves and others by drawing conclusions from their experiences. They attach an experience, including what is said to them, to a meaning that they create in their minds. Some of their beliefs will be empowering for them and some will be limiting or even damaging. What is lucky is that just as we are susceptible to forming limiting beliefs, we are just as susceptible to positive suggestions for believing something more useful. Sarah's story is a great example of this.

I want my children to develop a positive and realistic self-image. I don't believe that we should praise children for everything, because then they lose touch with reality. When they go out into the world, it will not help our children to think they are good at everything, just as it doesn't help children to think they are good at nothing. I want to nurture a realistic self-awareness of their strengths and encourage them to develop those strengths and interests in order to build confidence.

In my childhood, actually saying that you were good at anything was considered immodest, or even boastful and actively discouraged. It is not very British to think you are good at something! It took me until I was in my thirties to say I was good at a particular thing and believe it, despite other people telling me again and again that I was. I believed that saying that I was good at something was immodest to such an extent that I found it difficult to say it even to myself.

The way we speak to children about their skills and behaviour has an enormous impact on the beliefs they form about themselves.

You are more than your actions: Identity, beliefs and behaviour

There are important distinctions between addressing an individual at the level of their identity or beliefs as opposed to their behaviour. Here's an example:

Jonnie causes trouble in the classroom. He flicks paper clips at other desks, makes other children laugh in the class, doesn't concentrate for more than a few minutes at a time, and pulls faces at the teacher.

Consider the impact of the following statements:

> "Jonnie, you are a rude boy". This is a statement of identity – who Jonnie is. This is a generalised statement that Jonnie may identify with and start to live up to.

> "You think you can do anything you like in the class, don't you?" This is a statement at the level of belief – what Jonnie believes about his role in class. This is an extremely unhelpful statement to make for several reasons. First, it is a guess, so unlikely to be accurate. Second, he may decide that it is a good way to think and again live up to it.

> "You are a troublemaker."

Again, this is a statement of identity.

Labelling children in a negative way "he's the naughty one" sticks, and human beings are fantastically good at living up to the labels. They become self-fulfilling prophecies.

As children get older and continue to identify with the labels assigned to them, their choices become more limited. Here's what I mean: "I can't help it; *it's just the way I am*." As soon as someone believes that a certain way of behaving is part of their personality, they believe they can't change. I know people who were labelled bullies at school and continue to behave that way at work, well into their adult life. When they start to think of their behaviour as being *bullying behaviour instead of being part of their personality*, it creates possibility for change. You can change your behaviour if you want to, can't you?

The Amber Zone

A friend's young, adopted son had just started school. He was four years old.

Her son had had a challenging life until he joined his new family when he was three. He understandably had some behavioural problems. Jane worked really hard to provide him with a loving and supportive family life and to help him catch up on his language and social skills.

He started to get into a few scuffles with classmates in the first two weeks of school. The school had a discipline procedure that involved having different coloured zones in the classroom. If the child behaved well they sat in the green zone, then they moved to the amber zone if they behaved badly and if they persistently behaved badly they sat in the red zone. As a result of his scuffles, he had been moved to the Amber Zone. Every day after the move, at least one of his classmates has said to him, "that means you are a naughty boy."

Let's think this through. This process will work well with children who do not want the teacher and the other children to think badly of them. These children are likely to already have good control over their behaviour and will see the zones as a deterrent to bad behaviour and a motivation for good behaviour. These are the type of children who would probably behave well most of the time.

This process will work with older children too, for whom public disciplining and labelling is a deterrent. In fact, Jane tells me that it is so well established that some of the older children send their parents into the Amber Zone at home! If this is anything to go by, most older children can cope.

How useful, though, is this process for a four year old? How useful is it for this little boy to be labelled as naughty *by his peers and the school system* in his first three weeks at school? I find it totally unbelievable.

What do we do instead?

We need to give children negative feedback in terms of what they did, their behaviour, not what that makes them. "Flicking your rubber at me was a silly thing to do" is very different from "You silly boy."

Let's return to Jonnie. Here are some behaviour level statements that we could use:

"Jonnie, you are distracting the other children. You are making them laugh which means they can't concentrate."

Consider the difference in these statements:

Identity		Behaviour
You are a bully	vs.	You are bullying Fred
He's so naughty	vs.	He behaves badly sometimes

Giving children identity level feedback needs to be empowering for them. "You are kind," reinforces a kind act, for example. Like everything else, it is important to think about the possible consequences of whatever statement you are about to make. Sometimes we hold on to beliefs that we formed about ourselves when we were young which limit us in some way as adults.

I'm sure that you know people who are good at something but really believe that they are not. You may be like that yourself. We invest an enormous amount of energy in proving that we are right about it, sometimes in the face of overwhelming evidence to the contrary which we dismiss as a " one-off" or "fluke." Wouldn't it have been great if we hadn't formed those limiting beliefs in the first place?

You can help your children to not form limiting beliefs by challenging statements that they make about themselves and others that you consider unhelpful. Children come out with alarmingly sweeping statements that need to be nipped in the bud.

"I'm no good at anything."

"I must be stupid if I can't do this."

"I don't like Henry any more because he doesn't get things right at school."

Knowing what you know from Chapter 6, you have the questions to challenge these.

1 "I'm no good at anything."

What do you mean you are no good at anything? How does not being good at *this* mean that you are no good at *anything*?

2 "I must be stupid if I can't do this."

How does not being able to do *this*, make you stupid?

3 "I don't like Henry any more because he doesn't get things right at school".

How does Henry not getting things right at school cause you to decide that you don't like him anymore?

The next step is to make a positive suggestion that provides them with evidence that their statement is not true.

1 "I'm no good at anything."

What do you mean you are no good at anything? How does not being good at this mean that you are no good at *anything*?

Positive suggestion: Let's think of all the things you are good at. You're good at . . .

2 "I must be stupid if I can't do this."

How does not being able to do *this*, make you stupid?

Positive suggestion: You can't do this YET because you are learning.

3 "I don't like Henry any more because he doesn't get things right at school".

How does Henry not getting things right at school cause you to decide that you don't like him anymore?

Positive suggestion: Do you think that if you didn't get something right then people wouldn't like you? Of course not. Not getting things right straight away is part of learning, and you and Henry are both learning.

Summary

- Listen out for positively and negatively phrased language.

- Have a go at rephrasing negative instructions into positive instructions.

- Think about your beliefs about yourself and your children.

- Give negative feedback in the form of statements about behaviour not identity.

- Think carefully before assigning a label to a child. Will it empower them or disempower them?

- Listen out for your child's limiting statements about themselves and others.

- Challenge limiting statements with questions and make positive suggestions.

8

How DO they do THAT?

Strategies for success

We all want our children to have success. Success means different things to everyone. For me, my children will be successful if they achieve what they want to in their lives and are happy doing it.

If we want success in our lives we need to be aware of what we do well. We need to know specifically how we do something well so that we can keep improving it and do it more often. If we want success in our lives we also need to know what we do less well. We need to know how we do those things less well so that we can stop doing them or change the way we do them to a way that works better. If we want our children to learn effectively we need to teach them ways of learning that they find useful.

My father was very good at maths. I remember him trying to help me with my maths homework as a teenager. The experience was deeply frustrating for both of us. I simply could not make sense of the way he approached the problems. What I realise now is that his way of thinking through the problems was completely different to my way of thinking. Neither of us was consciously aware of *what* was different in our thinking and we certainly didn't have the ability to find out. In fact, we weren't even remotely aware of the possibility; we just knew that we did it differently and got frustrated. If only I had known then, what I know now.

We have already covered in detail how to find out how our children create some of their problems. We already know that if we are trying to help a child get over a problem, we need to know how they are representing the problem in their mind before trying to help them.

In this chapter we are going to use the same skills to find out how our children do other things – not just how they create problems for themselves – so that we can help them increase their self-awareness and make learning fun.

The word **strategy** describes how we do what we do. It is a combination of the things that we do that can be observed by others and what happens in our thinking, usually a series of internal representations that influence our physiology, state and behaviour. All this leads to a result of one sort or another, whether it be successful or less than successful.

Everything we do has a strategy, whether we know it or not. We have a strategy for brushing our teeth, for getting dressed, for remembering where our car keys are and for complex tasks. Some of our strategies are very effective and some are less effective.

We aren't consciously aware of most of our successful strategies because they are second nature to us, the strategy is operated at an unconscious level. As a result, if we are really good at something and someone asks us how we do it, the chances are we won't be able to tell them. Not easily anyway.

I would love to know how some people can look in the fridge and construct a fabulous meal out of whatever is there. How do they know that it will taste good; how do they know how much of each ingredient to add; how do they know how long to cook it for? All the answers to those questions are in the mind of the individual, and very possibly out of their conscious awareness. If we were to ask them how they do it, they would probably say, "I just do it" or "I just know."

In sport, psychologists are employed as a matter of course to help sportsmen with their "inner game"; their mental state. At the top level, it is, more often than not, the athlete's mental state that makes the difference between winning and losing.

The great tennis champion, Roger Federer, reaches shots that astound commentators who say that it is not human to be able to reach shots in that way. Roger Federer says that he does it by *putting the game into slow motion*. How on earth does he do that? I wonder if anyone knows his strategy for slowing down time.

As useful as it is to find out strategies like this, it is also enormously valuable to be able to discover strategies that are less than useful and are therefore hindering performance, like Tom on the football pitch.

The children's problems that we have looked at so far were all generated by individual strategies that were hindering their performance. A few of the children in the examples were suffering from anxiety of some sort. Anxiety is a good example of a simple strategy.

How we do anxiety

Here's how it works. We make pictures of the future going wrong in some way. Remember Alice who was going to take a tap exam and was making pictures of the examiner looking like a witch, which caused her to feel anxious.

Often we hear people say, "But what if I don't pass?" or "What if they don't turn up to meet me?" In order to say those things they have to have imagined it happening. That then triggers a feeling of anxiety. People who spend a lot of time worrying are very good at imagining negative things happening to them and then imagining the next negative event as a result of the first, followed by the consequences of that one. This is not a strategy for a happy life.

Take a moment to think about something that you were once worried about, or something that you are slightly worried about now. It might be an event that you are organising, something at work or even something small like being concerned that someone will not like the present you have bought them. How are you imagining the future in relation to the issue that is causing you concern? What pictures are you making? Are there any sounds associated with it?

Worrying about every day events is part of human nature. However, it is not useful if it keeps you awake at night, interferes with other things you have going on in your life, or, most importantly, gets you an outcome that you don't want.

Getting over anxious moments

A child's imagination is a powerful thing. It is the foundation for play and creativity. It is also a fertile ground for creating anxiety, worrying and negative thoughts.

Here are some simple ways of getting rid of the anxiety and worry. They are easy to teach to children too. My children use these strategies on their own now, consciously, if they are worried about something.

All these ideas involve changing, in some way, the internal representation that is creating the negative state.

1 Make an image of the event going well.

If someone is dreading a presentation, it is common for them to make images of a stoney-faced or heckling audience!

Instead they can replace this image with a smiling and applauding audience.

Try it out for yourself. What's the difference in the feelings that are attached to both pictures?

Or, they may have an image of themselves metaphorically going to pieces. They can change that image to one where they look and sound confident and relaxed.

If one of my children is a bit anxious on their way to school or going out somewhere, I ask them to get a picture in their head of them skipping happily into school or enjoying the trip. It has an instant effect.

2 Make the negative image comical in some way.

The solution for Alice and her anxiety about her examiner looking like a witch was to turn the witch into a giant teddy bear! End of anxiety.

J. K. Rowling demonstrates this technique in *Harry Potter and the Prisoner of Azkaban*. In the children's lessons they learn how to deal with their darkest fears. There is a creature called a Boggart whose true form can never be seen because as soon as it appears in front of you it turns into the thing you fear most. So if you fear spiders it turns into a giant spider. The young witches and wizards are taught to imagine making a comical change to the manifestation of their deepest fear whilst they cast a spell on the creature: "Riddikulus!" If they imagine hard enough, the creature in front of them will take on the comical changes. So the giant spider suddenly has roller skates. For any Harry Potter fans out there, it is easy for their parents to suggest to them that they make some comical change to the image that is causing them concern.

3   Push the image away.

Sometimes it is the vivid and close up nature of the image that is frightening for children.

When Thomas was three years old he started watching Disney videos. I have always been careful about what he watches as he has always been easily frightened by the smallest thing. In one particular week, he watched a bit of *Snow White and the Seven Dwarfs* every night. He absolutely loved it and I was surprised that he wasn't frightened by some of it.

One night as he was going to bed, he told me that he kept on thinking about the bit where the wicked Queen changes into the old woman and that he couldn't get it out of his head.

I asked him to look at the picture of the Queen again. This was a mistake as children of that age are so literal that he started to look all around him saying, "Where?" My second, and much more successful, attempt was to ask him to look at the picture of the wicked Queen *in his head*, which he did straight away without question. I asked him if he could make the picture go further away. What he then did surprised both of us for different reasons; he *literally* pushed the picture away from him with his hand and immediately started laughing. When I asked him what happened he said that the Queen fell over and that she wasn't frightening any more.

It may sound odd to ask, "What happens inside your head" but I have found that it makes more sense to younger children than "mind" or "thoughts." Now, whenever Thomas has frightening or unpleasant thoughts, he knows he can push them away.

Some variations we have used are: crumpling up the picture as if it were paper and throwing it away; changing the qualities of the picture, for example turning the sound down or putting a silly voice in; and occasionally he asks me to push the picture away "because your arms are longer than mine"!

4 Act as if they have control of their images.

Theo and his brother Tom were sleeping in the same bedroom when Tom woke up from a nightmare. Theo woke up with the commotion and gave Tom this advice: "When that happens to me I just imagine I have a remote control and I change channels." It worked.

Discovering your children's strategies

Getting curious about how your children do something well has so many benefits. It increases their awareness of their internal processes so they can apply the same strategy to other things; they can share what they do with other children to teach them excellent strategies; it makes children aware of the learning process – something that the school system does not, currently; and it is a great way of learning more about your child. Here's an example of a successful strategy:

Thomas's story

Thomas is a fast runner. He is tall and strong and so he is built for it. I think a lot of parents dread sports day; it brings back memories for me of always coming in last (I am not built for speed!) and a horrible over-competitiveness inherent in everything, especially the parents.

When all the new parents turned up for the first sports day, there were quite a number of us who were worried about how the school would handle it. One hears horror stories of over-competitive parents – one school I know has banned the parents' race because so many of the parents were cheating (talking of great role models) – or weeping children, devastated that they came last. Thankfully, I was delighted to discover that the school conducted the sports day in a relaxed, fun, inclusive, non-threatening and encouraging way. And competitive too. I am not someone who believes that we must protect our children from competition. So, I must confess I was also surprised and a little delighted that Thomas turned out to be such a fast runner. He won all the straight running races and was even seconded to the year above to run for his house in the relay. Proud parents indeed!

Some time afterwards I decided to elicit his strategy. It turned out that he has a strategy for achievement, modeled from great leaders and taught in leadership courses all over the world.

We had not taught him that; he has it naturally.

So how do we find out our children's strategies, both useful and not useful?

There are three key steps to any strategy:

1 The starting point or the trigger – what is it that sets the strategy off? How do they know when to start the strategy?

2 The steps – these are the steps of the strategy that include their behaviour and what takes place inside their mind.

3 The end of the strategy – how do they know when to stop?

How to discover a strategy

The most important thing is to make sure that you are in the coaching states of curiosity and open mindedness. It's important that you stay interested and non-judgemental.

1 First, we need the starting point.

Ask "How do you know when to start ... ?" Or "What happens just before you ... ?"

2 Then we need to know the strategy.

Keep the questions simple. Keep watching their eye movements to give you clues and guide your questions. Remember that if they look up when you ask them the question they could be remembering the pictures they made at the time.

It is very important to pay attention to their eye movements because the questions are not always easy for them to answer. If you notice that they are accessing sounds, for example, you can prompt them by asking what they are hearing.

"What is the first thing you do ... ?" "What is the first thing that happens?" "What did you do in your head/mind?" "What did you start thinking?"

Keep asking "Then what happens ... ?" until you think you have the whole strategy.

Repeat their strategy back to them. It should be logical. Imagine doing the strategy yourself to see if it makes sense.

3 How do they know when to stop?

Most of the time this is obvious and you don't need to ask. Just be aware that there is an end to every strategy.

Sam's story

Sam was a typically moody teenager, up one minute and down the next. He was able to go from really enthusiastic to sullen and rude in a moment. His family got pretty fed up with not knowing when he was going into one of his bad moods, and when he was in one, not knowing how to deal with it. They tried ignoring him, getting cross, and everything in between including asking him why. They didn't get anywhere, until one day his father tried a different tack.

Here's how he found out Sam's strategy:

Dad: *Sam you are really good at getting yourself into one of those moods. I am interested, HOW do you do it?*

This question threw Sam into some kind of confusion, but his father persisted with an attitude of genuine curiosity. Sam really had to think about the answer and was surprised himself when he eventually came out with the following:

Sam: *Well, I think about someone I don't like.*

Dad: *And then what do you do?*

Sam: *Well, then I look at the ground and walk like this…*

At this point Sam demonstrated rounded shoulders, and dragging feet.

Dad: *So first you think of someone you don't like, then you look at the ground, then you round your shoulders and drag your feet. Is that right?*

Sam *[surprised]*: *Yes.*

Try it. It's enough to put anyone into a bad mood!

Sam's father now has his strategy for getting into a bad mood but he doesn't yet have the trigger – what causes him to decide to go into the bad mood in the first place.

If asked the right questions, Sam might be able to become aware of what sets him off. And if he becomes aware of what it is that sets him off, he straight away has more choices in the moment.

The question for Sam is: "What happens just before you start thinking about...?" Or, "How do you know when to start getting into a mood?"

Sam: When you ask me to do something I don't want to do.

Finding out how Sam got himself into such bad moods so often was a breakthrough for the family. It had been extremely tiring for them all to try to manage his moods. Sam had gained new awareness which had opened up choices for him. As he was now conscious of how he created the bad moods, he couldn't really do them as effectively any more because he realised what he was doing and found it amusing!

It also enabled Sam and his Dad to have a conversation about Sam's response to requests; a conversation that simply was not open to them before.

Let's look again at a successful strategy: Thomas and his running.

Here, I had in fact guessed the start point of the strategy; the line up to the race. So my first question was about the steps of the strategy.

Me: What happens inside your head when you are standing on the start line about to run a race?

Thomas: When I'm standing like this? (He got into the "ready" pose!)

Me: Yes, when you're standing like that on the start line, waiting for the whistle.

Thomas: I make a picture of me running across the line first with my arms up in the air.

I could have asked, "And then what happens?" but that wouldn't have made sense. The race was over in his thoughts in the first piece of the strategy. It is a very simple strategy.

So it was purely out of curiosity that I asked him whether he said anything to himself to go with the picture:

> **Me:** Do you say anything to yourself when you are standing on the line?
>
> **Thomas:** Yes. "I will win."

Hannah has a less successful strategy as I discovered: "I say to myself, 'I probably won't win this.'" And she's right!!

Encouraging children to be curious about each other's strategies

Eliciting children's successful strategies is a great way to learn about learning and get children interested in how each other does things.

We were on holiday with some friends and I was with the four children sitting on a wall waiting for someone to join us. To pass the time, one of the children suggested that we did some sums – they were still at the age when adding and subtracting had some novelty! All of them thought it was a great idea, amazingly, so I duly set about firing simple sums at them in turn. Then something happened which surprised and delighted me. One of them asked the others how they did the sum in their head – and they proceeded to elicit each other's adding strategies! And because children are naturally curious, their conversation was peppered with; "Gosh, I don't do it like that, I do it like this ..." and "I'll see if I can do it your way."

The four children effectively shared their strategies and started to work out which one worked best. Imagine what would happen if that happened in classrooms round the country.

Helen's story

Helen (14) was having extra lessons for maths. When the maths teacher asked her what had brought her to these lessons she said, "I can do the easy sums but not the difficult ones." There is a great deal of information about her strategy in that one sentence. For example, how does she decide that something is easy or not? How does she decide it's difficult?

Instead of just teaching her how to do the difficult sums, the maths teacher did something much more effective. She decided to find out her strategy for doing easy sums.

She asked Helen to do an easy sum on the list. She did it immediately and the teacher asked, "How did you do that?" Like most of us, Helen had no conscious awareness of her mental strategy so replied, "Well, I just knew it." Not to be beaten, the teacher explained that we have a strategy for everything, even getting out of bed and cleaning our teeth, and that some of the steps in the strategy are things that we do and some of the steps happen in our mind. She explained that even if you think you just know something, you have been through some very quick mental processes to get there.

So she tried again.

Teacher: *When you look at that sum, what's the very first thing that you do in your head?*

Helen: *Oh yes, I have a picture of the two numbers in my head so that I can decide which one is bigger.*

The teacher carried on with this line of questioning, "And what's the next thing that happens?" and so on until she had Helen's entire strategy written on a piece of paper.

The next step was to try out this strategy on the "difficult" sums. The teacher asked Helen to choose the most difficult one on the page. Despite protestations from Helen, they methodically applied her strategy to the difficult sum and managed to get to the right answer quickly and easily.

Helen now knew how to do all the difficult sums and had learned how to do it by becoming aware of her own mental processes. How much more motivating and inspiring that is for the child than trying to teach them how to do a "difficult" sum. Brilliant.

In the next chapter, I will share some useful strategies for spelling, maths and comprehension.

Summary

- A strategy is the process by which we do what we do.

- Try changing your child's internal representation in some way if they are anxious.

- Elicit your child's strategies so that you can tell them how they do what they do well.

9

Understanding learning; learning understanding

When I work in business, I encounter adults who have negative associations with learning. Some seem defensive or worried about learning new things and about putting themselves in any situation where they don't already know how to do what I am asking them to do. Others, who also have negative associations with learning, say that they already have the skills that the workshop covers, despite clearly demonstrating that they do not. It seems that "not knowing" is seen as a weakness by some and creates anxiety in others. This attitude to learning obviously affects their ability to learn new things so they continue to do what they have already done. Learning passes them by.

How can we prevent children from growing into adults with these negative beliefs about learning? As we know they may have formed them from their parents or other important adult figures in their lives like teachers. We, as significant adults in our children's lives, are role models whether we like it or not. It is best then that we model beliefs that will be useful to them in their lives. And the most interesting and successful people that I have met have common beliefs about people and learning.

They believe that:

- We are always learning.
- All things are possible.
- All outcomes are results of some kind.
- All of us have potential.

Let's look at those in more detail. What do they mean to us?

1 We are always learning. People who believe this believe that they can always learn something from any situation, however familiar it is to them. They believe that today they will be better than yesterday and tomorrow they will be better than today in respect of their knowledge and skills.

2 All things are possible. People who have this belief think that if someone can do something they can too, as long as there are not any obvious physical restrictions. For example, it would be unrealistic for a fifty-year-old man to believe that he could become an Olympic high-jump champion.

3 All outcomes are results of some kind. To have this belief means that you learn from your mistakes instead of considering that you have failed. Thomas Edison is an often-quoted example of someone who held this belief. It took him thousands of attempts to produce the first working light bulb. He considered that each failed attempt was another way *not* to do it, so with each one he knew he was closer to success. He never considered that he had failed.

4 All of us have potential. Everyone is capable of more. Everything we need to be successful in our lives is within us.

I am extremely privileged to know lots of inspirational people who have these beliefs. The most inspiring teacher I know runs a Montessori nursery that my children were lucky enough to attend. She has an enormous amount of wisdom, gathered over her many years of teaching. I asked her what her beliefs are about children. This is a précis of what she said about the way she approaches teaching:

- Make it clear who you are and what you stand for so that the children know.
- Give of yourself and let them come to you when they are ready.
- Never laugh at children even if you think they are being sweet and never make slighting remarks.
- Let them know that you notice everything they do because you care. If they think that you are all seeing and you encourage good behaviour, they will behave well to please you.
- All negative behaviour can be changed.
- Learning is exciting, so think about what is exciting for them and teach them that.

135

- Encourage listening skills by giving them something interesting to listen to. Then when you ask them to listen, they will.

- Keep watching and listening. Never think you know what they are like, because children surprise us all the time. Don't allow yourself to be surprised.

Wise words. I know teachers who make these beliefs explicit in their classrooms to encourage children to embrace learning. Imagine what school would be like if *all* teachers had these beliefs and were able to help children form these beliefs too.

Currently, I find myself questioning the validity of an education system where the priorities are so focused around results and testing that children who start school at four with an air of excitement and curiosity find themselves at the tender age of seven thinking school is boring. What are we creating for adulthood if our school system manages to achieve this in three short years? I find it incredibly sad that we are knocking curiosity and fun out of our children when they are so young.

Time for a change in thinking.

How useful it would be if our school system encouraged life-long learners. And yet, I have met newly qualified teachers who say that they learned almost nothing about learning in their teacher training that was useful to them. The information was overwhelmingly biased towards content.

There is so much wonderful information available on learning and getting the best out of different learners; there is even more information about managing behaviour and delivering lessons in really effective ways. Whether or not new teachers get access to all of this is down to their placements – are they lucky enough to be able to model teachers who are excellent, or are they placed in a school where the teachers are less interested in trying out new ideas?

There are lots of great teachers who are working with cutting-edge learning and communication strategies with their pupils. It seems that there are also plenty who are not. This is why it's important that we as parents learn to understand our children and understand the process of learning so that we can help them learn and develop effective strategies and challenge the system if we find that our children are not learning.

What is learning?

Learning is a crucial part of a human being's ability to function successfully in the world. Learning is an active mental process. You cannot make someone learn, they have to take an active role in it themselves. It involves being able to make meaning from our surroundings and from information we are given by building on what we already know, and working out how to apply what we have learned in the future. The more actively involved we are in the learning process, both mentally and physically, the more we will learn. The more we are encouraged to think about what we are learning, the more it sticks. If you cannot make sense of what you are learning, you will not learn.

Making sense of learning

What does comprehension mean? Comprehension means understanding. That is, our ability to make meaning from something. New information needs to be related and attached to information that we already know in order for us to make sense of it.

We can help children learn by starting with something they already know, their background knowledge, and attaching the new information to that in some way. Gaps in understanding occur when the child is unable to attach the new learning to their own experience. Have you ever been in a situation where someone has explained something to you which you simply could not understand? That happens because you have no internal reference experience to attach it to. Sometimes, as they keep talking, you make sense of it; it clicks. Your mind has been actively searching for something to attach the new information to and has suddenly found it.

The best teachers are those who know this and relate every new piece of learning to something that is familiar to the whole class. They speak the language of the pupils and use analogies and anecdotes that everyone can understand.

When I think back to my psychology degree, I cannot believe the amount that simply went over my head. You can probably guess that I was very interested in the subject and therefore highly motivated to learn. I now realise that there were some tutors who were incredibly knowledgeable about their specialist field and yet could not translate their knowledge into language that made it real for a group of undergraduates. Despite being highly motivated to learn, I found some of the subjects difficult to understand.

On the other hand, there were other tutors who connected the subjects to our previous knowledge and to real life so well that I remember almost everything they taught, even now. I think it is quite a feat to manage to teach a subject like psychology and *not* relate it to real life!

The question is: *how* do people make meaning? We are back to our internal representations again. If I were to ask you what the word "door" means you would immediately be able to tell me. So how do you know what it means? You probably have an image of a door in your mind, or an explanation of the function of a door, or you may look around the room for one. The fact is that we all create our own internal dictionary or reference for all words.

Some words are much more difficult than others. How do you know what "was" means, for example? I would guess that you know what it means in the context of a sentence. I used to wonder why children, when they first learn to read, find some two or three letter words difficult; they were simple to sound out so how come they stumbled over them? I realised that they all had something in common; they were abstract in some way, and therefore difficult to "picture": was, in, on, and, but, the. In spoken language, those words are always in context for the child, so they only become tricky when they stand alone. As a child reads more and more, they get to understand the meaning of words like these through putting them into context.

A child who is good at comprehension, then, is constantly referring to their internal dictionary and making connections between that and the text as they are reading. When very young children first learn to read, they have reading books that have a high ratio of pictures to words. This aids comprehension; that is, the word "car" goes with a picture of a car. As readers get more competent, the amount of pictures in books decreases and they have to make internal pictures to help them understand the story.

One of the symptoms of dyslexia is difficulty with comprehension. Also, there are some children who are able to read perfectly well, and can not answer comprehension questions on the piece they have just read. In both cases, the children have not made the connection between the words on the page and their own internal reference. These same children can understand a story that is read to them perfectly well. Isn't that interesting? It's not that they can't understand a story, it's that they are unaware of their internal processes that enable them to understand. It means that the process that they use to understand the spoken word is not utilised when they are reading.

There is of course more to think about when we read something ourselves. We have to concentrate on reading the word and making sense of it at the same time. I am working with an adult who finds reading novels very difficult for this reason. He is practising reading a sentence, stopping and asking himself, "How do I know what that means?" He is practising making full internal representations after each sentence so that he connects with the story.

How can we help our children to make the connection?

Like everything else, the first step in helping anyone is to help them become aware of their internal processes. And in order to help them become aware, you need to get really interested in how your child does what they do.

A simple question which helps children become aware is to ask them, "How do you know what that means?" You will notice what they do with their eyes; are they looking for pictures, hearing sounds, talking to themselves or accessing feelings? The most effective internal dictionaries are mostly visual as you can hold much more information in a picture. If you are not sure what they are doing, ask them or prompt them.

Here's a conversation I had with a child who is mildly dyslexic and whom I was helping with comprehension.

> **Me:** How do you know what the word "table" means?
> **Jane:** It's brown.

I could see that she was finding a picture in her mind through looking up. I also knew that she was accessing a visual image because she said that it was brown. Telling me that it is a certain colour presupposes a visual representation.

> **Me:** What's the difference between an old table and a new table?
> **Jane:** The old one is a bit raggedy and the new one is shiny.

Again, Jane was giving me visual qualities in her answers.

> **Me:** So you know what those words mean because you have a picture of them in your head.
> **Jane** [looking a bit surprised]: Yes, I do.

Jane was now aware of her internal processes for comprehension. I also asked her about more abstract words and we made up silly sentences for her to remember.

Then we moved on to her current spelling words for school. For each word, we did the visual spelling strategy for the actual word and attached meaning to it through deliberately creating a mental image or sentence to go alongside the word. For each word we did the following:

Write the word out on a separate piece of paper in a colour of the child's choice.

Me: What sort of colour would the word "right" be?
Jane: Pink

We wrote the word out on a separate piece of paper in pink.

Me: How do you know what "right" means?
Jane: I don't really know.
Me: Well I imagine a big tick with the word "right" beside it.
Jane: Oh, I was thinking about me with an arrow on my head pointing to the right!
Me: Great! It means that too.

So for each word, we did a drawing, symbol or contextual sentence to concrete the meaning.

Jane was learning how to do this for herself every time she got a new list of words. She also realised that it would be a good idea to stop and think about the words when she was reading. This allowed her time to find her internal reference for the meaning, rather than focusing so hard on the actual word that all comprehension was passing her by.

Jane and I spent just over one hour together learning these two strategies: how to remember the spelling and how to remember the meaning. Her mother has told me that her confidence has improved tremendously, she spends approximately a quarter of the time learning her spelling and is consistently getting most of them right, and she is choosing to read more often which has led to a big improvement in her reading ability. She told me that Jane volunteered to read aloud in class, which is a big step.

Summary of comprehension strategy

- Help your children understand words and prose by encouraging them to make mental images. If necessary, draw pictures for them that explain the meaning.

- Ask, "How do you know what that means?" to help them become aware of their internal dictionary.

- When explaining something new, connect the new subject to something they already know.

Every day, children with borderline problems are labelled as dyslexic because they are not reading as effectively as their peers; they don't spell very well, or they have comprehension problems. In my experience, some of them simply do something in their internal processing that blocks their ability to spell or read, or they miss something out in their internal processing that is crucial to performing the task effectively. In other words, they have strategies that don't work that well. They may not be dyslexic. A child I know is being sent for dyslexic testing because "she is reading only at her reading age". Her reading age is spot on and she is being sent for a diagnosis?!

Imagine how useful it would be if *all*, rather than just some, teachers were taught to be aware of children's learning strategies. What happens at the moment is that those pupils whose learning strategies match the teaching methods do well, and those whose don't, don't. Those pupils who think differently get sent for diagnosis to see what's wrong with them. In fact, some children unwittingly get taught out of a naturally occurring useful strategy and into one that works less well. Spelling is a fabulous example of this.

We now know that all excellent spellers have the same way of knowing how to spell a word thanks to the work of Robert Dilts.* He interviewed expert spellers and observed that they had remarkably consistent eye movements when asked to spell a word. The vast majority of them looked up and to the left of their visual field, which indicated that they were accessing a visual memory. They saw the word in their mind's eye. When he asked them how they knew the word was spelt correctly, they replied that they *had a feeling that it looked right*. They saw the word in their mind's eye and immediately got a feeling of familiarity if it looked right.

Try it for yourself. Choose a word to spell and notice how you know how to spell it. If you are a good speller, you will notice that you see the word in your mind's eye, probably in the top left hand corner of your visual field. (Remember from the eye chart on page 62 that this is the place for most people's visually remembered information). If you are not aware of this, try spelling it backwards and you may become more aware of the appearance of the word.

To be able to spell really well, Robert Dilts discovered that it is *essential* to have a visual internal representation (in this case a memory) of the actual word. If you consider yourself to be a less good speller, notice how you try to find the word to know how to spell it. Do you sound it out, perhaps?

Robert Dilts found that the most common strategy of poor spellers was to try to spell the word through sounding it out phonetically. Phonics has an important role to play in learning to read but it is not a useful way to learn how to spell. This is particularly true for English as there are so many words that are not spelt phonetically. Ironically, "phonics" is one of them. This excellent spelling strategy can be taught to just about anyone; after all, we are all able to visualise.

* Robert Dilts has been a developer, author, trainer and consultant in the field of Neuro Linguistic Programming (NLP) since its creation in 1975. He has spearheaded the applications of NLP to education, creativity, health and leadership. You can read more about his work on his website *www.nlpu.com*.

Currently, the way our children are taught to spell at school means that, although it works perfectly well for the majority, some children find spelling difficult when they don't need to. This is why:

If we want to remember a word, we have to store it in our visual memory. Our visual memory is accessed by looking up and to the left (for most of us). Those of us who visualise easily, store words there, naturally and unconsciously. The national curriculum way of learning spellings is: Look, Say, Cover, Write, Check. Children who visualise easily (which includes the majority of children), will automatically file the word in their visual memory as they write out the word again and again during the week.

Those children who do not naturally file the word in their visual memory struggle with this way of learning spellings. They need to be told to make a picture of the word. They need to understand that if they want to remember a word they need to look up to unlock the file.

There is no provision for making sure that the word is remembered visually because looking at a piece of paper on the desk means the child is looking down. This means that for children who do not automatically put the words in their visual memory, this is a much less effective strategy.

One of the other reasons that children find spelling difficult is the insistence that they "sound it out". This teaches them to have an auditory strategy which doesn't work effectively. The vast majority of dyslexic children that I have worked with have some sort of auditory strategy.

Whilst explaining the visual spelling strategy to a group of adults on one of our workshops, one of them suddenly exclaimed, "Oh that's why I remembered some words better than others. My grandmother used to label all the pieces of furniture to help us remember what they were called and how to spell the word. I always wondered why I remember the ones that were *above my eye line* better than the others. Now I know!"

Making spelling easy

Below, I describe how to teach the spelling strategy to your child.

The Spelling Strategy

1. Use your child's current weekly spelling list.

2. Find out where they look when accessing visually remembered information. Use the eye movement game to help you. For most of them it will be up and to their left.

3. Explain to them that it is easiest to remember pictures when their eyes are pointed in that direction (with head facing front).

4. Ask them to think of something that they are confident and familiar with. It is very important that they are in this positive state so that when you show them the first word it will automatically become associated with "familiarity" instead of any negative state that learning spellings might be associated to.

5. Write the first word on a plain piece of paper in a colour chosen by them. It is easier and more fun to remember things in colour.

6. Hold the word up in front of them, in their visual remembered field.

7. Put the piece of paper down and replace it with a plain piece held up in their visual remembered field. Ask them if they can still see the word on the plain piece of paper.

8. If the answer is "Yes," take the plain paper away and ask them if they can still "see" the word in their mind. If the answer is "No" go back to point 6.

9. Ask them to spell the word backwards. They can tell you or write it down. If they write it down, make sure that they go from right to left so that the word is correctly spelt when they have finished – we don't want to create a nation of children who can only spell in reverse. The purpose of doing this is so that you can check that they really can see the word. If they can not see it, they will not be able to do it. It is almost impossible to sound out a word backwards.

10. If they do it correctly ask them to spell it forwards.

11. Explain to your child that when they want to remember the word again, they simply look up and to the left (or wherever their visual remembered accessing is) and see the word. If they can't remember how to spell a word, just look up and wait for it to appear.

Note to teachers: It is extremely useful for younger children to be reminded during spelling tests that they should look up to find the correct spelling of the word.

Adapted from *The Spelling Strategy* with kind permission of Robert Dilts.

This strategy has been around for a long time now. There is research that consistently shows this strategy to be more effective than any other strategy that is taught to our children. It is my mission, and the mission of many others, including many teachers, that all children are taught this way as a matter of course.

Experiment with your child. Go with your instinct and if they are finding it less than easy, make suggestions: make the word more colourful, bigger or smaller, chop the word into chunks if it is a long one. Ask them to guide you as to what helps them. Build on success.

Children are amazing. I asked one child if she could see the word in her head and to spell it backwards. She said that she could see it but that it was too far away to read. I asked her to make the word come closer. She immediately said, "That's better, yes I can read it now," and spelt it correctly!

I have personal experience of children with real difficulties in spelling ability being helped beyond what they thought was ever possible by learning this new strategy. I have watched mothers' jaws drop as their young son or daughter spelt a word backwards that twenty minutes earlier they had no idea how to spell. I have heard stories of children, diagnosed with severe dyslexia, having their lives changed by this simple technique of visualising words.

So, the spelling strategy is a small but significant example of how understanding internal processes, and teaching effective ones, can open up new possibilities.

Naomi's story

Noami is a thirteen-year-old girl who had been labelled as severely dyslexic and was very unconfident. She knew that she struggled but was desperate to be given the chance to get into the A set for the GCSE syllabus for English. Her new dyslexic teacher taught her the spelling strategy and in only half an hour she was able to correctly spell complex words backwards and forwards. The teacher told me that Noami was so overwhelmed at her improvement that she was almost on the ceiling with excitement! They were both in tears (of joy) at the end of the lesson and it really has changed her life.

Making times tables easy

We are encouraged to help our children learn their times tables by chanting. This is useful up to a point. Mental arithmetic requires us to "see" the numbers so it is more useful to teach children to memorise their times tables and formulae by visualising them.

The Maths Strategy is the same as the spelling strategy. It is useful for remembering times tables and formulae that you need to know off by heart.

The Maths Strategy

1. Use the appropriate times table or formula they need to remember.

2. Find out where they look when accessing visually remembered information. For most children it will be up and to their left.

3. Explain to them that it is easiest to remember visual information when their eyes are pointed in that direction (with head facing front).

4. Ask them to think of something that they are confident and familiar with. It is very important that they are in this positive state so that when you show them the first sum it will automatically become associated with "familiarity" instead of any negative state that learning maths might be associated to.

5. Write the first formula or sum (8 x 6 = 42) on a plain piece of paper in a colour chosen by them. It is easier and more fun to remember things in colour.

6. Hold the sum up in front of them, in their visual remembered field.

---

7. Put the piece of paper down and replace it with a plain piece held up in their visual remembered field. Ask them if they can still see the sum on the plain piece of paper.

8. If the answer is "Yes," take the plain paper away and ask them if they can still "see" the sum in their mind. If the answer is "No" go back to point 6.

9. Ask them to tell you the sum backwards. The purpose of doing this is so that you can check that they really can see it.

10. If they do it correctly ask them to do it forwards, always looking in their visual remembered field.

11. Explain to your child that when they want to remember the sum again, they simply look up and to the left (or wherever their visual remembered accessing is) and see it.

Adapted from *The Math Strategy* with kind permission of Robert Dilts.

Keeping our children motivated to learn

As learning requires active involvement from the learner, it follows that motivation to learn is vital. If a child, or an adult for that matter, is bored or demotivated in some way, they will not learn. Helping children to be in a positive and motivated learning state is as important as the information they are being given.

What motivates us to learn?

Think about the last time you chose to learn something new. What was it that got you to start learning?

Were you just interested in the topic? Were you inspired by someone? What relevance did it have to your life? What were the positive consequences of learning it? Perhaps you just thought it would be fun.

Floyd's story

My husband, Tim, used to run an organisation dedicated to helping young people with significant learning difficulties to find employment. This involved teaching them the necessary social and technical skills required for a whole range of trades. Floyd was one of these young people. He was a small and slight sixteen-year-old who had managed to find his way through the education system without it apparently having had any impact whatsoever. He was largely illiterate and innumerate and suffered, as a result of being bullied, from an extraordinary degree of defensive behaviour, to the extent that he was hardly able to communicate verbally with anyone other than his peers. One day, Floyd was taken ill and his supervisor, Ken, drove him home. Floyd was so grateful to him that he, amazingly, invited him into his house and asked if he would like to see his room. Ken could hardly help but notice that the walls were covered from floor to ceiling in posters of motorbikes and on the floor were piles of motorcycle magazines.

At that moment he realised the key to Floyd's motivation. He asked him to bring in his magazines, which he currently couldn't read, and designed a programme of literacy and numeracy based around motorbikes.

Six months later, Floyd could tell you the cost of the petrol required to ride a 600cc Yamaha from London to Newcastle and back – a not-inconsiderable feat of mathematical skill – and six months after that he entered his first full-time employment in the warehouse of a vehicle parts supplier.

Floyd's story is a dramatic one but the same thing happens every day in schools to a degree. Thomas really lost interest in reading when he was given a certain series of books. He was simply not motivated to read because he didn't find them interesting. When I asked his teacher to give him some books that were more interesting to him, she told me that he needed to read the ones he had been given to consolidate his reading skills and that they were part of the required stages. You may be able to imagine my response to that. How was he going to be able to consolidate his reading if he wasn't interested? Is it not more important to keep a six-year-old interested in reading by giving them something else to read than stick rigidly to the curriculum and risk them losing interest in reading altogether?

Remember how easily children generalise from their experience. It doesn't take long for a child who has lost motivation for reading certain books to generalise that all reading is boring. And boredom is not a useful state for learning.

Charlotte's story

Charlotte gets easily distracted at school. She notices everything that is happening around her, the trees blowing outside the classroom, other people talking, anything. This has a major impact on her learning and her class work.

When she started extra lessons, her teacher noted that she had no concept of the consequences of not concentrating. It had been explained to her many times but she was just not getting it. Her teacher noticed through her eye movements, her physiology and through questioning, that she was talking to herself all the time. So of course she didn't hear the teacher's instructions or explanations. Her auditory channel was already full of her own conversation with herself!

Her teacher decided to show her the consequences of not concentrating, using the visual and kinaesthetic channels, thereby by-passing the auditory channel. She showed her how learning takes place through demonstrating the building of knowledge with the analogy of a brick wall. When she had put a few bricks in place, she showed Charlotte what would happen if she stopped concentrating at that point thereby creating a gap in the brick wall. She then asked Charlotte to guess what would happen if she tried to put more bricks on top of the hole in the wall.

"Oh no – the whole wall could come down!" Charlotte had immediately realised the impact of allowing herself to be distracted in relation to the greater consequences for her learning.

This understanding of consequences meant that her motivation to concentrate in lessons increased dramatically.

What can you do at home to increase motivation for learning?

- Be enthusiastic and interested in learning – it's catching.

- Look for learning opportunities in everyday activities.

- Increase your child's awareness of their internal processes through asking questions and demonstrating curiosity.

- Make the most of their preferred mode of thinking. If your child has a visual preference, explain through drawings. If they have an auditory preference, focus on sounds to get them interested. If they have a kinaesthetic preference, engage them in some physical activity. Best of all, use all three channels if you can.

- Connect the new learning to something they know already.

- Always relate the learning to real life. What's useful about knowing this or being able to do this skill?

How does mood affect learning?

You will remember from the communication process that a state is a physiological state, which we label according to what we are doing and how we are thinking at the time. We usually label this "emotion."

The state of excitement is almost identical to nervousness, from a physiological point of view. If you have a positive internal representation of a forthcoming event, you are likely to label your internal sensations of butterflies as excitement. If you have a less positive internal representation and are imagining something going wrong, you may label it as nervousness. You will also remember that state affects behaviour, always.

It is extremely important for children to be in a positive learning state when they are at school. Negative feelings inhibit learning and positive feelings accelerate it. When I think back to being at school, the lessons I learnt most from were the ones that the teacher made fun, challenging and enjoyable in some way.

Children learn well when they are:

Curious

Open to new ideas

Motivated

Relaxed

Happy

Comfortable

Excited

Engaged

Challenged

Children do *not* learn well when they are:

Bored

Nervous

Stressed

Anxious

Fearful

Lacking in confidence

In an over-competitive environment

Negative

Anxiety and fear of failure

In my work I often come across adults who do not want to ask questions in a learning environment for fear of looking stupid; I used to be like that myself. And there are many who will not answer a question unless they know they are going to get it right.

Fear of looking or sounding stupid inhibits learning.

Let's be clear: there is no such thing as a stupid question. Any question means that you are trying to make sense of something, which means that you are learning.

As parents we must encourage our children to ask questions and always make them feel OK about it. If our children are going to grow up into confident adults, they must get the message that if they don't get an answer right, that's OK, they can just keep searching for the answer.

We need to challenge teachers and other adults who do not have this attitude and who make children feel bad for getting things wrong.

Children learn when they feel safe and confident and when they can build on success. Children do not learn when they find a situation threatening. Anxiety inhibits learning, even when a child is motivated to learn.

I have already mentioned how we make ourselves feel anxious; we construct an internal representation of things going wrong, or otherwise failing in some way. If we are worried about failing, our attention will be on not failing, more than it will be on achieving the task in front of us. The state of anxiety also releases chemicals into our system that inhibit our ability to think, and therefore to learn.

Kate's story

One of my sisters, Kate, is dyslexic. This is how, in the mid-1970s she learned to hate reading and despise books.

153

She vividly remembers English lessons at school aged 9 or 10. Every child was required to read aloud to the class. This is how Kate describes the experience now:

"I dreaded English lessons to the point that the whole lesson was a write-off. The whole experience was akin to ritual humiliation. I knew at some point in the lesson, I would have to read out loud. We did it in the same order every time and as we got closer to my turn I got breathless, my heart would race to the point where I could hear a pounding in my head, my vision was impaired and I felt dizzy. I would take deep breaths to try to calm myself down but the nerves would keep building so that I literally heard nothing except a muffled sound of far off talking which was actually my friends reading in turn. Despite the fact that in this high state of anxiety I couldn't actually hear the words, I could hear the fluency of the words, and the gap between their ability and mine reinforced my lack of confidence and my belief that I was a failure when it came to reading.

"When it got to my turn, I remember looking at the page and seeing a sea of words swimming about in front of my eyes, the lines all merging into each other. I was focusing so much on pinning the words back on to the page, and keeping the lines separate, that it was impossible for me to hear the sentence I was reading; I could only try to stagger my way through each word hoping to get away with as much as possible. After reading about a fifth of everyone else's turn I was asked to stop and thankfully the relief overshadowed the shame, until my whole class was given my mark out of 10; normally 2 for effort."

Unsurprisingly, Kate has never enjoyed reading. Since having children of her own, she has regained some confidence, but she still suffers from anxiety if she has to read in front of another adult.

Even though I'm sure these kinds of experiences happen less and less, our school system still encourages children to fear failure, fear getting the answer wrong, and fear looking or feeling "stupid." Some teachers and parents value "getting it right" over "having a go." If children do not feel supported in taking the risk of having a go they will learn to fear failure.

I know a five-year-old child who is so frightened of her teacher that she cries on waking and pleads with her mother every morning not to take her to school. How effective do you think her learning is in that state? It is unacceptable that any child of that age is frightened of the teacher. Learning happens most effectively when we feel safe, not threatened.

Anne's story

Anne is one year away from taking her GCSEs.

She is very eloquent in class, but when she is asked to write things down in exams she just cannot get the words on to paper. She gets into a state of high anxiety and as a result can't think straight. She believes that she has something wrong with her mind that means she can't write her thoughts clearly which is in itself contributing to the anxiety.

When I elicited her strategy for getting herself into the state it was as follows:

1 She already feels anxious before she goes into the exam because she believes that she will find it difficult.

2 She then looks at the paper and says to herself, "Oh my God I have to fill that piece of paper."

3 Then she looks around and sees other people writing and starts saying over and over again, "I must start writing."

As a result, she cannot access any memories that she needs in order to take the exam because her thoughts are full with her talking to herself.

There is nothing wrong with her mind. She needs to learn how to access a positive state when she takes an exam.

So how can we help our children to access positive states?

Ways to help your child get into a positive state for learning

1 Through asking questions

Eliciting a positive state in someone is easy if you know what questions to ask and if you are in a resourceful state yourself. One friend of mine who has started using these simple techniques with her children after coming to one of our workshops said, "It really is just about using your brain to work out what you want and being a bit more creative in getting it." Exactly.

The quickest way to change someone's state is to ask them what it is like for them to be in the specific state that they want to be in. The reason this question works is because in order to answer it they have to access the state first. Try it for yourself.

- What's it like when you are confident?
- What's it like when you are happy?
- What's it like when you are . . . ?

You can't help feeling the emotion, can you? So whenever you want your child to experience a particular state, ask them this question.

A word of warning! We have found that this question works more effectively than other similarly worded questions such as, "What does it *feel* like when you are confident?" They simply don't work as well, so stick to asking,

- What's it like when you are ...?

Look up!

Notice the physiology of your child when they are in a bad mood or other negative state. It is highly likely that they will look down (remember the eye charts) in order to maintain the state, even if they are not aware of this. They may be talking themselves into the negative state too which also involves downward eye movements. They may also have rounded shoulders and general slumped appearance.

Robert's story

Robert is very good at "hamming up" a bad mood on the way to school. Knowing what you know, you would guess correctly that he looks down at the pavement whilst saying to his mother, "I really don't want to go to school, Mum. I hate school." As his mother knows that this is a bit of an act, she can quickly move to the future state, and elicit one that is useful for Robert to go into school with. So she asks him to look up at the sky.

This, in itself, will break his bad mood as he can't maintain it for long without looking down to refresh it!

When he looks at the sky she starts to ask him to make pictures about things which she knows he is looking forward to. "Robert, can you imagine playing with your friends at break time?" "Oh yes", he says, and immediately looks more positive and quickens his pace toward school!

Once Robert is looking in the direction of his visual field, it is easy for him to make pictures in his mind of the things that his mother knows he enjoys; in this example, playing with his friends in the playground. Now that he has a positive internal representation, his state changes too.

Let's just think back to Sam the teenager. He was excellent at getting into bad moods and could even describe how he did it. "I think of someone I don't like, talk to myself about them and look at the pavement." After checking that he wanted to have a different experience, his father suggested he looked at the sky as he was walking along. Sam was really surprised at the difference that made to how he was feeling.

3 Help them to create a new internal representation

In Robert's example, his mother not only got him to look up to change his state, she also asked him to create a new internal representation.

Creating a new internal representation can be as simple as asking your child to think of an activity that they find fun. So for example, I ask Hannah to think about herself tap dancing. As she loves it, I know that if she accesses a memory of tap dancing, it is likely that she will end up in a positive and receptive state.

I quite often ask the children to get a picture of themselves really having a fun time when they are in their class learning, or to make a picture of themselves concentrating well, listening well, learning easily, and so on. They do it quickly and easily, it takes seconds, and it sets their focus for the day. Not only does it make it extremely likely that they will behave in the way that they have mentally rehearsed, it raises their confidence about learning. This short exercise achieves so many things – it also means that they are constantly getting a message that learning happens easily and naturally.

4 Storytelling, guided fantasy, metaphor and meditations

Storytelling is an excellent way of eliciting states.

Stories go straight to the most powerful part of our mind, our unconscious mind. As well as using stories to elicit states we can use them for any number of things. While we are consciously paying attention to the story, our unconscious mind is making connections and meanings at a deeper level. That means that stories are a fabulous way of helping children learn and get positive messages about themselves.

Stephen's story

Stephen is the deputy head teacher in a secondary school for pupils with emotional and behavioural difficulties. At the school there are a lot of young men who demonstrate aggressive behaviour; they get into fights easily and also direct their anger at themselves. Stephen is extremely dedicated to his job and has those beliefs about learning that I outlined at the beginning of this chapter, which help him to be a great teacher, always looking for new ways to improve his own abilities and therefore improve the experience of the boys he teaches.

He came to study with us to see if he could find some new approaches to help him teach and manage the young men in his care. After the first module of the training, during which time we spent some considerable time on "state affects behaviour" Stephen went back to the school motivated to try things out. He decided that he would really concentrate on state. After the very first day back at school, he left a very excited message on our answer phone.

He told us that he had started the day with a guided relaxation fantasy. He had taken the boys on an imaginary trip to a tropical island with a cool breeze and warm sun. He took them through all the senses, what they might see (palm trees, clear blue sky, glistening turquoise sea, for example), hear (rustling of the trees in the breeze, the lapping of the waves on the shore) and feel (the warm sun on their skin, the sand between their toes). The boys responded very positively; they all managed a deeply relaxed state and remained a lot calmer than usual for a lot more of the day. One boy was very moved by the experience. He thanked Stephen, remarking that he had never been that relaxed in his life before.

5 Music

Playing up beat music in the mornings is a great way to get everyone feeling energetic and ready for the day; or alternatively, calming music for those who are already a bit over-excited in the mornings!

6 Games and physical movement

It has long been known that learning is an active process and we learn more effectively if our whole body is involved. For some children this is crucial. At the extreme, children who have a strong kinaesthetic (feelings and action) preference for learning are sometimes labelled as slow learners or as disruptive because of their need to move around.

As you know, state and physiology are linked, so it follows that if you change your physiology, you change your state. I'm sure that all of us have been in a situation where we felt that we needed to go for a walk to help us feel differently about something. And how often do our best ideas come to us when we are in the shower or bath when we are really relaxed? My best ideas come when I am on the running machine at the gym when I reach a trance-like state – the ideas seem to come from nowhere. They don't of course; they come from my unconscious mind.

Physical activity, then, is a great way to get into a state that is useful for learning particularly if you have a child with a strong kinaesthetic preference.

Trampolines are particularly good because bouncing uses so many muscle groups, is rhythmic and encourages a connection between mind and body. If you have a trampoline, you can combine all sorts of physical and mental activities to great effect. Try doing weekly spellings or times tables with your child whilst they are bouncing or walking around.

Nancy's story

A dyslexic teacher that we know, Nicola, made the most difference to her 12 year old pupil through working with her state. She noticed, in the first lesson, that when she asked Nancy to read to her, her state changed. Nicola paid attention to her physiology: shoulders going up, generally tight muscles, shallow breathing and flushed skin. In this state, Nancy's attempt to read was not particularly successful. Instead of ignoring her state, Nicola decided to work on changing that in preference to working on her reading skills. She asked Nancy to stop and asked her what happened when she asked her to read to her. Nancy replied that she immediately felt tense and panicky.

*In the coaching model, this panicky state is the **Present**. Nicola knew that she needed to get Nancy into a state that would be useful for her in the future. She decided that it would really help Nancy if she could get her to feel relaxed and confident.*

Nicola asked Nancy "What's it like when you are relaxed?" She kept asking her more questions like "How do you know? Where do you feel it? What are you thinking about?" and kept watching for changes in her physiology. She did the same with "confident" when she noticed Nancy relax. Nicola made sure that Nancy was aware of the internal pictures she was making to help her feel that way so that she could suggest to Nancy that she could think of this when she needed to be in that state, relaxed and confident.

When Nancy was in a really positive state, she asked her to read to her again. Nancy could not believe the difference in her ability to read; she could see the words more clearly on the page and hear her voice more clearly.

The effect of working on Nancy's state snowballed. Reading more fluently to Nicola helped her feel more confident and feeling more confident made her read more fluently. Soon, she surprised her teacher by agreeing to read aloud in class.

If Nicola had not known about the importance of state and behaviour, she would not have paid as much attention to it. In her opinion, she would have taken a lot longer to make progress with Nancy.

Thomas and his homework

Some children are obviously very happy to do their homework; some are not. Thomas is not. In fact when he started school, he quickly objected to doing extra reading at the end of a tiring day. Frankly, I didn't blame him. It seemed a bit much to ask a four year old to do homework, even if it was only for five minutes. I began to get concerned when he consistently went into a very negative mood when I suggested reading, as he was beginning to associate reading with the bad mood. I knew that if I allowed that association to continue much longer it would affect his motivation and ability to read, potentially for the rest of his life.

He was finding reading difficult and an all round negative experience. Every time I said, "Let's do some reading," his shoulders would slump and he would go into a very bad mood.

What I needed to do was make sure that he got into a positive emotional state when I asked him to read. So I decided to act out the story as he read. The story was one about an alien losing its socks, so it made for some hilarity as Hannah and I put our best efforts into acting it out. Thomas thought it was very funny so we did it again the next afternoon and the next one. By the third afternoon Thomas wanted to do his reading before I asked him to. After that we didn't need to act it out either, thankfully.

His reading improved quickly after that because he was in a positive learning state when he started, instead of a state that blocked his learning and improvement.

Try reading a novel when you feel in a terrible mood. It is very hard to concentrate and to understand what you are reading.

A bit about state and memory

Psychologists know that information learned in a particular state will be most effectively remembered and used in the same state. If you are feeling on top of the world, that feeling will trigger memories of lots of other times when you felt that way. The same thing happens with every other emotion; sadness, joy, understanding, confusion, confidence and so on.

Therefore it is most useful to learn something in the state that you will need to recall it. Students who revise in test conditions, perform better in exams than those who don't.

Creating the atmosphere of an exam or test, be it for ballet, music, spelling, or anything else, gives our children the best possible opportunity for performing well in the test.

We learn to drive a car by driving it, not by being told how to drive it. The sooner we can put new skills to the test, in the situations where we will need them, the better.

Summary

- Learning is an active process. The more we are asked to think about and practise what we are learning the more effective our learning will be.

- Learning will only take place if the new information or required skill can be connected to something the learner already knows and understands. If it cannot be connected, no learning will take place.

- Help your child's understanding by getting to know what they already know and are interested in and relate the new learning to that. Present the information in a fun way.

- Help your children to get motivated to learn using the ideas on page 151.

- People need to be in a positive state to learn effectively; anxiety inhibits learning.

- Encourage your child to ask questions by being positive about all questions. Help them to believe that all questions are useful.

- Help them to believe that not getting it right is part of the pathway to learning.

- Teach your children strategies for learning which teach them how to learn, rather than what to learn.

- Get interested in their strategies for learning to make them aware of unconscious processes.

- Share your successes at home with your child's school in a positive and supportive way.

- Help your child to get into a positive learning state before school.

- Learning something in the state and environment closest to the state that the learner needs to be in when recalling and using the information or skill makes learning most effective.

10

What do we do next?

Making the changes

We now know that if we are going to help our child think differently, we need to understand how they are thinking and what they want. So far, we have concentrated on the knowledge and skills needed to find that out.

If we do not spend time finding out how our child is creating their problem in their internal representations we can, at best, only guess how to help them. If we do not spend time finding out what they want, we can only guess at solutions. The **Future**, what we want, may be instantly obvious, in which case we know almost without thinking how to get there. Or it may be less than clear, a place that we know is different to the one we now occupy but as yet not clearly defined, in which case we need to do more to define it.

This chapter demonstrates how we can apply the coaching framework to guide our thinking in all sorts of circumstances.

The first seven stories bring the examples from Chapter 6 to their conclusion. As you read them, you will notice how sometimes change occurs *very* quickly and easily. I still get surprised at how easily change can happen. The more time and effort you put into finding the thinking behind the problem the quicker the change will take place.

You will also notice how the Coaching Framework created the understanding, the context and impetus for change and the stories demonstrate how you can take this thinking and apply it wherever and whenever you want.

The remaining stories in this chapter allow you to experience further examples of this way of thinking in action.

Laura's story revisited

Laura was very upset when she discovered that her best friend Betty would not be with her when she went into her new Year 3 class. Her parents did not actually know what she was thinking that was causing her to be so upset. They needed to know the content of her internal representation before they could really help her. What did Laura imagine would happen as a result of her best friend, Betty, not being with her?

Through questioning, her parents discovered that Laura was upset, not because of Betty, specifically, but because she thought that she wouldn't have anyone to talk to.

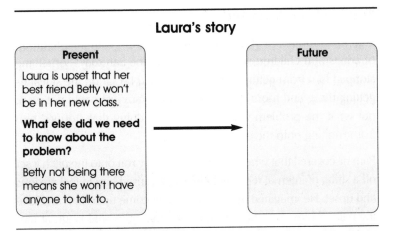

Laura's story

Present

Laura is upset that her best friend Betty won't be in her new class.

What else did we need to know about the problem?

Betty not being there means she won't have anyone to talk to.

Future

What does Laura want then? She wants to know that there will be someone to talk to when she gets into the new class.

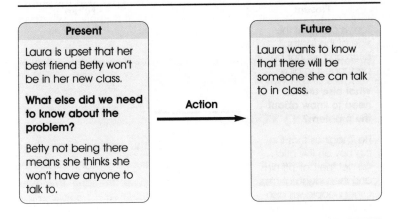

Present

Laura is upset that her best friend Betty won't be in her new class.

What else did we need to know about the problem?

Betty not being there means she thinks she won't have anyone to talk to.

Action

Future

Laura wants to know that there will be someone she can talk to in class.

What action can her parents take to make this happen for Laura?

Action

Her mother organised a number of playing visits with the girls in her new class over the summer holidays. Laura got to know three or four of the girls in her new class and started the term feeling confident.

Tom's story revisited

Tom loves football and was desperate to join in with a large group of adults and children who were playing one Saturday. Something stopped him from getting onto the pitch and he sat on the sidelines getting more and more upset. His mother Pam just could not work out what the problem was. What was he doing that stopped him from running onto the pitch?

Pam discovered that when he saw the big boy run onto the pitch it set off a string of internal representations that caused him to feel anxious and upset. He imagined that the boy might come up to him and take the ball off him. And then he imagined that he would laugh at him until he cried and that other people would then laugh at him too.

Tom's story

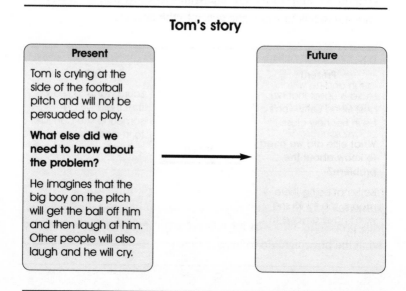

WHAT DO WE DO NEXT?

Pam started to challenge his problem thinking by asking him how he knew that that was going to happen. The result was that he started to doubt the validity of the problem.

Now Pam moved to the **Future** and found out what he wanted to happen.

> **Pam:** What do you want Tom?
> **Tom:** I want to play football with everyone.
> **Pam:** Are you sure?
> **Tom:** Yes

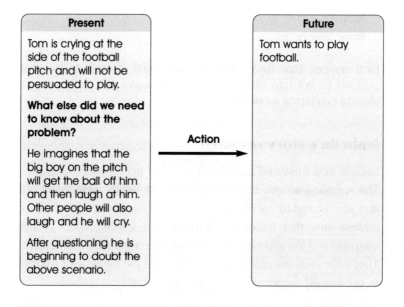

Present	Future
Tom is crying at the side of the football pitch and will not be persuaded to play.	Tom wants to play football.
What else did we need to know about the problem?	
He imagines that the big boy on the pitch will get the ball off him and then laugh at him. Other people will also laugh and he will cry.	
After questioning he is beginning to doubt the above scenario.	

(Action →)

Pam was sure that Tom wanted to play football and the thing that was preventing him was his internal representation of the boy and what the boy might do to him.

Action

He needed to change the picture. Pam created a new scenario for him to play as a film in his mind.

> **Pam:** Tom, let's change that picture you have in your head so that you can have some fun. What do you think?
>
> **Tom:** OK
>
> **Pam:** Can you make a picture of yourself running on to the pitch and tackling one of the dads and getting the ball off them?
>
> **Tom** [smiling]: Yes
>
> **Pam:** That would be good wouldn't it?
>
> **Tom:** Yes!
>
> **Pam:** What else can you imagine happening that would be fun?
>
> **Tom:** I could try to score a goal too!
>
> **Pam:** Very good!

Pam noticed that Tom's state had changed enough to be in a position to get him onto the pitch. She knew that once he was playing everything would be fine.

Isabella's story revisited

Isabella gets frustrated and loses control of her temper sometimes. The specific example was a day when the family were going out and she refused to get dressed. Although Susan does a good job of making sure that Isabella understands the consequences of her tantrums and the effect on other people, she continues to have them. They have even discussed what they want in the future – for Isabella to get dressed quickly when asked, without having a tantrum.

Isabella's bad behaviour continues because Susan doesn't have the crucial missing piece of Isabella's internal strategy for getting into a state like that. She doesn't know what *causes* the tantrums and asking her to stop having the tantrum is intervening in Isabella's tantrum strategy much too late. What she found out was that Isabella seeing her clothes is the trigger that makes her realise that she needs to make a decision. Then her mind goes blank which makes her frustrated. The more she is put under pressure the more frustrated she gets.

Isabella's story

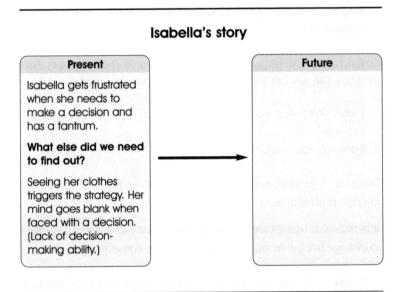

Present	Future
Isabella gets frustrated when she needs to make a decision and has a tantrum. **What else did we need to find out?** Seeing her clothes triggers the strategy. Her mind goes blank when faced with a decision. (Lack of decision-making ability.)	

Now Susan knows what she needs to do.

So what would be the agreed outcome to fit into the **Future**? What does Isabella need that would mean that she would not get frustrated and not have a tantrum?

Isabella needs a decision-making strategy. If she had one, it would interrupt her strategy for having a tantrum. This is how they agreed the outcome:

Susan: You don't want to carry on having tantrums do you?
Isabella: No.

Notice that Susan's statement is phrased in terms of what she doesn't want, so she needs to rephrase it.

Susan: So let's think about what it would be like if you behaved well when I asked you to get dressed. Can you get a picture of you making a choice easily and putting the clothes on?
Isabella: Yes.
Susan: So what would that be like if you did that?
Isabella: Fine.

Susan has asked Isabella to mentally rehearse the outcome. And next she can ask her to think through the consequences.

Susan: And what would happen next if you got dressed nicely in that way?
Isabella: You wouldn't be cross with me.

What do you notice about Isabella's answer here? What is her internal representation of the consequences?

It is of Susan being cross. If Susan wants Isabella to feel compelled to change her behaviour, she needs positive consequences too.

Susan: So if I "wouldn't be cross with you" what would I be instead?
Isabella: You would be pleased with me.

That's a more useful internal representation. Susan can take this one step further to get Isabella more connected to that statement "You would be pleased with me." Here's how:

Susan: And what's it like for you when I'm pleased with you?
Isabella: I like it.
Susan: And what else happens?
Isabella: We have a good time together.

Susan spent some time making the **Future** compelling for Isabella. Going through this process helps Isabella to feel motivated to change her behaviour because she has rehearsed the positive consequences of behaving well. So now all that remains is for Susan and Isabella to agree to the action which is to learn how to make simple decisions.

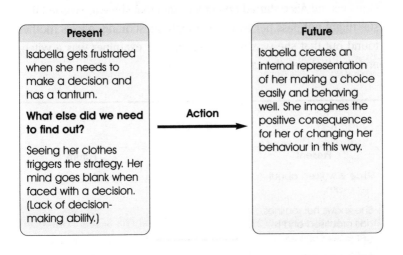

Present

Isabella gets frustrated when she needs to make a decision and has a tantrum.

What else did we need to find out?

Seeing her clothes triggers the strategy. Her mind goes blank when faced with a decision. (Lack of decision-making ability.)

Action

Future

Isabella creates an internal representation of her making a choice easily and behaving well. She imagines the positive consequences for her of changing her behaviour in this way.

Action

They decided to learn some good ways to make decisions. They agreed to make it a project for Isabella to find out how her friends made decisions to see if she could adopt their strategies.

What did making it a project do for Isabella? It gave her responsibility for changing her behaviour and learning something new. It also meant that she needed to go and ask her friends some questions about their strategies which taught her about being interested in other people's internal processes. As a by-product she learned about how to learn, even though she would not have any conscious awareness of that. Some pretty amazing side effects!

Alice's story revisited

Alice was about to take her first tap dancing exam. She knew all the exercises and routines, had practised like mad and loves it.

One evening Alice started crying and said that she was worried that she might not pass her exam. Through questioning, Alice's mother found out that she was imagining that her examiner was a witch, and that that was the cause of her anxiety.

Alice's story

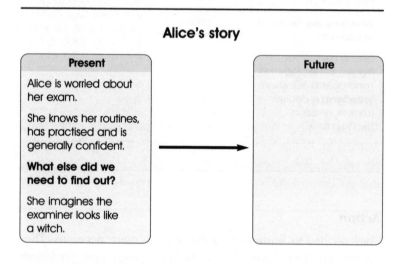

Present	Future
Alice is worried about her exam.	
She knows her routines, has practised and is generally confident.	
What else did we need to find out?	
She imagines the examiner looks like a witch.	

In Alice's case we do not need to spend time on the **Future** because it is obvious that she simply needed to think about the examiner in a different way.

What action should her mother take?

The course of action she chose was to ask Alice to change the examiner into a giant cuddly teddy bear, which worked brilliantly. Alice immediately started laughing and felt better.

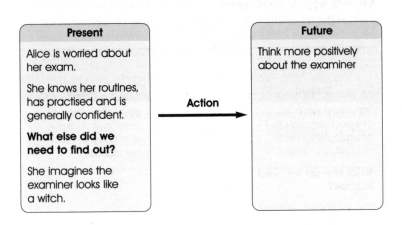

Tara's story

Tara, just 5, would not jump in to the pool on holiday despite really wanting to. As this had been going on for four weeks, I knew that she was imagining something pretty terrible happening. I discovered that she thought she would drown if she jumped in.

Tara's story

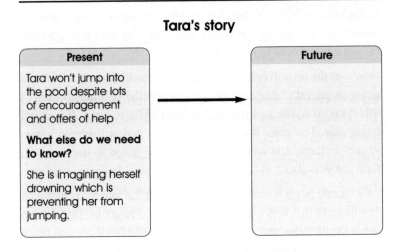

I already knew that she wanted to jump in because I had checked that she had the motivation to do it at the beginning of our conversation.

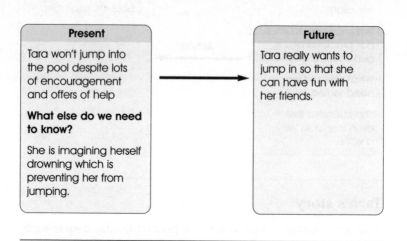

Present		Future
Tara won't jump into the pool despite lots of encouragement and offers of help	→	Tara really wants to jump in so that she can have fun with her friends.
What else do we need to know?		
She is imagining herself drowning which is preventing her from jumping.		

Action

Again, this was a case of the block being in her internal representation. To change her behaviour, I needed to help her change her thoughts.

So I asked her, "Can you see that your friends are jumping in and *not* drowning?" Of course she could easily see that, and that question helped her to doubt her own fear.

Now was the time to help Tara to create a new image – one that was going to get rid of her anxiety and give her the courage to jump. I asked her to make a picture in her head of herself jumping in and being safe. The great thing about children is that they can create images instantly and without question. I suggested to her that each time she was about to jump in she could make that same picture.

I also asked her if it would help if I stood in the water to catch her. She thought that was a great idea so I started to get in. Tara was so fast at creating the new image that when I asked her if she was ready to give it a go she just went ahead and did it, before I had time to get

176

in! Once she had done it once, there was no stopping her. She quickly had proof that she was going to be OK and had a great time with all the others.

Pam, Lucy and Luke

Let's go back to Pam who I told you about on page 42. She got very frustrated by her nine-year-old daughter, Lucy, getting dressed slowly in the mornings and thinking that it would make them late for school. As a result of realising what triggered her frustration, she was able to focus on what she wanted to happen in the mornings in order to make the changes. Here is her story in her own words:

"Mornings in our house were a complete nightmare. I used to scream and shout at the kids and tell them at least 25 times to do all the things that needed doing: teeth, hair, uniform etc. Needless to say this was very tiring and left both me and the children stressed and not starting the day in the way that I wanted to. I decided to take a look at the way things worked in the house and realised it was mostly my reaction to Lucy's relaxed approach that was causing the problem; my need to be in control.

I wondered what would happen if I told them what needed to happen in the mornings and by what time and let them decide how they wanted to do it. I sat them down and we all agreed that mornings weren't good and that things needed to change. I asked them if they were interested in trying a new way. They both agreed to give it a go so I gave them a list of all the things that needed to be done in the mornings and when they needed to be done by. I said that I would trust them to do it by themselves and that I would not remind them at all. We agreed that we would leave the house at 8.30am whatever state of dress they were in.

The following morning we started the new system. Luke, my six year old was completely ready by 8.00am and had time to do some drawing and have a chat about school. I was really pleased that things seemed to be working. However, when 8.20am came and Lucy was still not dressed I had to bite my tongue. It was very hard for me not to interfere and tell her to hurry up (nearly as stressful as shouting!) as I was starting to think that she might be going to school in her pyjamas. Then a small miracle happened: she disappeared upstairs and came down, ready to leave, at 8.30am.

I was very proud of them and told them so. It was a much better way to start the day and still is. I still don't understand why Lucy has to work under pressure and likes to leave things until the last minute, but I now know that it doesn't matter. I don't need to be in control of the way she works; she does it her way and I do it my way. The house is much more harmonious now that I think that way (most of the time anyway!)."

Pam's story

Present		Future
Pam got frustrated every morning when she saw Lucy getting dressed slowly and imagined that they would be late. As a result she shouted at the children leaving her feeling frazzled.	**Action** →	Pam wanted to feel calm in the mornings. She focused on what she wanted to happen in the mornings. She told her children specifically what needed to happen and by when. She also made clear the consequences of both achieving and not achieving this outcome.

The key thing here was that Pam set her children an outcome: what needed to be done and by when. She then allowed her children to work out how to achieve that on their own.

Sam's story revisited

Think again about Sam the teenager and his moods that he created so well.

With the help of his father's questions he became aware of his strategy. The next step was for his father to find out what he wanted. Simply, his father asked him, "Do you want to carry on being in bad moods and for the rest of the family to get fed up with you?"

"Not really," came the reply.

Next his father could find out what he did want, and what help he needed to stop him going into his strategy.

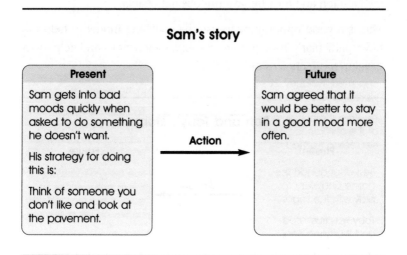

Sam's story

Present	Action	Future
Sam gets into bad moods quickly when asked to do something he doesn't want. His strategy for doing this is: Think of someone you don't like and look at the pavement.	→	Sam agreed that it would be better to stay in a good mood more often.

Action

His father suggested to him that when he thought he might go into a bad mood, to think about someone he liked and to look up – thereby completely changing his strategy. It worked.

Ben and Toby's story

Ben and Toby are eight-year-old friends who play together regularly. They have a bit of a love–hate relationship. They play together well until one of them decides they want to do something different from the activity they are currently doing. Ben says that he wants to play with the Lego and Toby still wants to play the Star Wars game that they have made up. Ben goes off to get the Lego out, leaving Toby in the midst of a game that he can't continue on his own. Toby's reaction to this is to go and thump Ben. Ben turns round and thumps Toby back and a scrap ensues.

The mother, Lisa, comes and tells them to play nicely and they carry on until the next disagreement. The boys learn nothing from Lisa's intervention and their behaviour does not change.

This is a good opportunity to use the coaching model to help the boys, particularly Toby, to think through their actions and help them develop more choices of behaviour.

Ben and Toby's story

Present		Future
Ben abandoned the game and went to play with the Lego.	**Action** →	
Toby was frustrated and thumped Ben.		

You can see here that Toby has not made the relationship between what he wants to happen and how he goes about trying to get it. We know what he wanted; he wanted Toby to carry on playing with him. Asking him about what he wanted to happen as a result of his behaviour is much more powerful as a tool for change than assuming he has made a connection and is just badly behaved.

Here's how their conversation continued:

> **Lisa:** What did you want Ben to do?
> **Toby:** I wanted him to carry on playing with me.

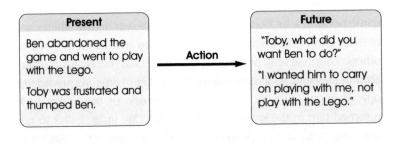

Present	Action	Future
Ben abandoned the game and went to play with the Lego. Toby was frustrated and thumped Ben.	→	"Toby, what did you want Ben to do?" "I wanted him to carry on playing with me, not play with the Lego."

Action

Now we can help him make the connection between his action and his intention or desired outcome.

> **Lisa:** Did you think that hitting him would be a good way to get him to play the game with you?

The point here was to get him to realise the outcome of his behaviour, which was to be told off and Ben not wanting to play, versus what he wanted. Then Lisa asked for suggestions for ways that he could have persuaded Ben to go back to the game. She also included Ben who gave Toby suggestions on how to persuade him.

What did the boys learn from this approach that they did not learn from just being told to behave? They learned to think through consequences of their actions, and to think about what they want *before* they act.

By asking Toby about what he wanted to happen, Lisa was able to relate his behaviour to his outcome.

William's story

It was the Easter holidays and we were at one of those soft play places that are heaven for six-year-olds. There were three boys playing together who were all school friends. At one point their game became a bit boisterous, and we were wondering when one of them was either going to get hurt or come and tell on one of the others. They had long pieces of sponge and were hitting each other around the head, so it really was only a matter of time. As predicted, one of them, William, came to say that one of the others had punched him in the stomach and the back. My instinct was to go and deal with the perpetrator. Instead, I followed the coaching model and asked him what he wanted me to do. He thought for a minute, smiled at us, shrugged, said "Nothing" and ran off.

What was the difference, then, for William, between my following my instincts and following the coaching model? The key difference was that by following the coaching model, William was invited to consider the reason for coming to tell us. I could tell by his final smile and shrug that he had got that message. I wonder what he will do next time.

Natalie's story

I met Natalie on a business workshop that I was running. I was teaching a group of senior sales executives how to use this framework as a sales process. Not only did they successfully incorporate it into their working lives, some of them phoned me with success stories from home. Natalie was one of them.

She has two sons, Constantin, 13 and Dimitri, 9. This is her story in her words.

"Last week, my eldest son came back home from school really angry and became aggressive with his brother. Dimitri was – for once(!) innocent and hadn't provoked Constantin. Instead of punishing him for his behaviour, I decided to ask him some questions. I was able to discover that the reason for this anger was a bad mark he had in school.

Practising my questions, I asked him, "What was it about getting a bad mark in school that has caused you to feel angry?" He replied that he was afraid of the punishment that he would get for getting a bad mark, as he had promised that morning that he had worked for his exam. Of course I would not punish him for getting a bad mark, only for promising something that wasn't true, so I was glad to be able to clear up that misunderstanding.

My usual reaction to news of a bad mark would have been to give him a long monologue on how tired I am with telling him the same things about working in school, the importance of getting a good level in class for his future, and the fact that he his more than capable of getting good marks when he concentrates on his school books more than on his Game Boy! Of course by repeating this once more I would have got furious with him again and sent him to his room without even listening to him or giving him a chance to talk.

I knew I needed to find out more so we calmly sat down together. I explained that I was really interested in helping him and finding out what was preventing him from preparing properly for his exams. I went through the process of asking questions using his words by "bouncing from an answer to another question."

I uncovered all sorts of valuable information: he admitted that he didn't feel comfortable with this particular teacher and that he didn't feel confident in the studying of this particular subject. We agreed an outcome together; he wanted to feel confident in understanding this subject. I asked him to think through the consequences of understanding it and what it would be like. He seemed to be really motivated by that.

Then we planned how we would achieve that together – what help he needed from me and what he needed to do to stay focused. He felt he was heard and respected. He even surrendered his Game Boy as a way to keep him focused during exam time. He called me to his room the evening after to study together. All this came from asking a few initial questions when he picked on his little brother, instead of making a judgement and sending him to his room. I feel we have made real progress."

Tracie and Phoebe

Tracie and her husband had separated a few months before and Tracie was having a very difficult time with her eight-year-old daughter, Phoebe. Phoebe is very bright and had been behaving well at school. However, for some time now, when she came home she had seemed very angry and directed all her anger at her mother, who understandably found it tough to deal with. Phoebe used abusive language and would not comply with her mother's wishes. As a result of months of this, her mother was tired and worn down by it and found herself responding negatively to Phoebe. She acknowledged that Phoebe probably thought that she didn't even like her as all her focus has been on dealing with Phoebe's bad behaviour at home. In comparison, Phoebe's little brother was "angelic."

This scenario is a good example of the whole family being so inside their problem that they had lost focus on what they wanted. All they knew was that they wanted it to stop and couldn't see a way out. Phoebe's mother found a way out by thinking about how they wanted to behave towards each other.

First they needed to acknowledge the **Present**. Tracie needed to explain to Phoebe that things could not carry on the way they were. She needed to point out specifically what they were both doing that was no longer acceptable. She also needed Phoebe's agreement that she didn't want their home life to continue in this way. Having done this, they were ready to plan together what they wanted to be different at home.

Phoebe likes drawing, representing things visually and finds articulating her emotions difficult, like most eight-year-olds. Tracie decided to ask her to draw a picture of what she would like her time at home to be like. Tracie drew one as well.

Phoebe found that easy to do. She felt that Tracie was really trying to understand her and it enabled them to start to think about what they both needed to do differently in order to make it happen. Thinking in this way together has had a positive impact on their relationship. Drawing is an excellent way of getting a lot of information when words don't quite seem adequate.

Thomas

Boys go through a testosterone-fuelled time at approximately seven years old. Both physically and psychologically this is a time in a child's development that is a milestone. As a result we had some pretty angry behaviour from Thomas that was generally out of character.

I got fed up with none of my usual approaches working; sending him to his room for a few minutes to cool off, talking through what had happened, imposing sanctions and even resorting to a version of a star chart that we hadn't done since he was about three.

One day he had been aggressive in a way that was particularly unusual. There was no alternative but to send him to another room to be on his own to cool off. I was very angry at his behaviour and in that moment was at a loss as to what to do. Then it came to me. I would ask him to write about what had just happened. Using the coaching framework as a guide, I wrote down some questions on a piece of paper, leaving a big space for him to write in under each one.

Here are the questions:

- What was my bad behaviour?
- What happened after I did it?
- What did I want?
- What is a better way of getting what I wanted?
- What will happen if I find a better way?
- What would be a good thing to do right now?

I asked him to answer the questions and to bring them to me when he had finished or if he had any questions. After about fifteen minutes he brought in his piece of paper and we went through his answers calmly together. There were some things I had to help him think through and he added to his answers.

This exercise had an extraordinary effect. The act of writing about his behaviour made him consider it fully and accept that he had indeed behaved badly. He had time to think about it calmly and time to come up with some alternative ways to behave without being rushed. I was proud of him for making so much effort to answer the questions and surprisingly he quite enjoyed the process. It turned out to be even more thought-provoking for him than being asked the questions. For me, it gave me time to get myself into a more useful state than "angry," so that I was well-equipped to help him learn from the experience, which he did.

Summary

- Solutions follow understanding.
- Get a clear **Present** and **Future** before offering solutions.
- Use this framework anywhere and any time to:
  - solve problems
  - think through consequences
  - change behaviour
  - set outcomes
  - determine action

Conclusion
A final few words

This book is about change, about creating a different "present" for ourselves and our children that in turn will lead to a different "future." My purpose has been to offer you a set of skills and, more importantly, a framework for thinking that will allow you easily and effectively to bring about that change and, in time, enable your children to bring about change for themselves.

Our children are magical beings and have the instinctive ability to create their own wonderfully rich internal worlds. Discovering how they create these and understanding their format and structure – their internal representations – has been our adventure together. This discovery has led us to the keys to the present: how they create problems, how these problems are formed and, equally important, how they create the other presents, the bright, compelling and successful ones.

Our adventure has also led us to thinking about the future. We will all at some time have dreamed, dreamed of the things that we want. All the evidence around us points to the fact that those people who have a clear vision of what it is that they want – and are motivated to move towards it – are far more likely to achieve it than those who do not. And so it is with our children and their futures.

I hope I have successfully demonstrated how you can take this thinking and apply it wherever and whenever you want. And that, of all the messages in this book, is the one that I would ask you to hold closest to your heart. Thinking in this way can and will change the way you interact with and experience your children. It will change the way that they experience you. And in that new experience the seeds are sown for a future full of discovery and wonder.

And one last story...

... not mine, but nonetheless dear to me, and which I have been told many times. In some way it crystallises my message to you.

Many years ago, a steam ship which, having been sailing the trade routes of the world for some years, had acquired a reputation for reliability. On all its voyages it had never once had any mechanical problems of any sort. Yet one day, as it was about to leave port, ready loaded and prepared for a voyage that would take it half way round the world, a problem of such severity developed that the engines failed and the captain was forced to abort the voyage and send for help. No-one on board could find the cause of the problem.

Residing in the port was an elderly engineer, with a reputation for being able to solve any problem that was put before him. The Captain sent for him and some while later he arrived, carrying a small bag of tools. "What's the problem?" he asked. The Captain explained as best he could and the engineer asked to be taken to the engine room.

Once there, he began a minute examination of the engines; he listened and watched carefully and occasionally would call for silence so that he might concentrate even more. After an hour he opened his tool bag and pulled out a small hammer. He walked over to a set of pipes and gave one of them a sharp tap. The engines sprang into life.

The Captain stood amazed. "Thank you, thank you," he said. "Tell me how much we owe you and we will pay you here and now."

The engineer looked up. "£101," he said. "£101!" the Captain exclaimed. "You've only been here an hour and used no materials and replaced no parts. What am I paying for?"

"£1 is for my time" said the engineer, "and £100 is for knowing *where* to tap."

191

Emma Sargent has spent the past fifteen years working as a trainer and coach with both corporate and private clients. She has acquired a reputation internationally as an extremely knowledgeable, effective and inspirational trainer.

Emma has a degree in psychology and is a certified trainer of Neuro Linguistic Programming (NLP). She co-founded Ambo Ltd with her husband Tim Fearon where they run workshops for corporations, parents and teachers as well as NLP Practitioner and Master Practitioner certification trainings.

They live in the New Forest with their two children, Thomas and Hannah.

Emma can be contacted at:

www.emmasargent.co.uk
www.ambo.ltd.uk